THE SILVER THREAD OF LIFE

50 Original True Accounts of Divine Interventions and Life-Changing Spiritual Events

By Phillip Bruce Chute, EA

While all the stories in this book are true, some names and identifying details have been changed to protect the privacy of the people involved.

First paperback edition February 2018
Second paperback edition November 2020

Book cover German Creative
Editing by Nenita Lariosa

ISBN (Paperback): 978-0-692-06056-8 (1st)
ISBN (Paperback): 978-1-7328855-2-3(2nd)

www.phillipbchute.com

DEDICATION

I dedicate this book to the wonderful people who bared their souls, who gave me their precious secret events that profoundly changed their lives and to my etheric guardian spirits for keeping me alive through a dozen close deaths to write this book. This spiritual journey continues forever for all of us.

I also dedicate this book to Troopers Von Schmittner and Cosby, for giving their all to an ungrateful unforgiving Army.

TABLE OF CONTENTS

TABLE OF CONTENTS

TABLE OF CONTENTS

TABLE OF CONTENTS

TABLE OF CONTENTS

Acknowledgment

Many thanks to my friends and clients who, like myself, have experienced the Divine Intervention and Spiritual events portrayed. God bless them and the readers of these stories.

Also, many thanks to Alayna Photography; Steve Holt, Comanche photographer and horseman; Anthony Nguyen, my outstanding intern; and for my beautiful supportive wife, Nanette who helped edit this book.

Preface

When I came home from the Army, I saw my family's tax returns on the kitchen table prepared by a lawyer. Because the family was renting out the second floor of the large home, it made the returns complicated. This was the first time I ever saw a tax return because, in the Army, the wages were so small that there was no need to file taxes. I noticed how the taxes and interest expenses for the house were split between Schedules A and E, but the tax-half was missing on one schedule. I showed it to my father, but he didn't understand. At the time, I would have never envisioned that this little happening would become the foundation of my career as an accountant and stock-broker-principal. The magic of my occupation is that I see hundreds of people every year, and they share their stories because they know me as a good listener.

This book, however, discusses only the world of real facts and stories experienced either by me or the people I know. My first book, *American Independent Business,* which became a college textbook, and *Rock & Roll Murders,* which was a true crime story, kept my feet firmly on the ground in criminal law and concrete experience. With imagination gone, washed away by hard years of harsh, grueling facts, I had nothing creative behind. Though, I must note that *The Far Side* is my favorite reading. My 2,000-volume library is gone from moving too many times, but it has been a pleasure to write this book from memory—not just tax code and legal facts. I have many professional awards in my office but the ones most important to me are the awards for writing. Perhaps, I have been kept alive all these years to bring this treasure for your enjoyment and for you to be able to find parts of the work that relate to you on a personal level. The events in this book are generally life-changing and have been kept secret for many years by their keepers. Now, you can experience their life-changes through your own mind's eye. After all, we all have secrets to tell.

Chief Seattle said it all in his beautifully eloquent statement regarding President Franklin Pierce's acquisition of tribal lands in 1854:

"This we know: All things are connected. Whatever befalls the earth, befalls the sons of the earth. Man did not weave the web of life: he is merely a strand in it. Whatever he does to the web, he does to himself. Every part of this soil is sacred. Every hillside, every valley, every plain and grove, has been hallowed by some sad or happy event, in days long vanished. Even the rocks, which seem to be dumb and dead as the swelter in the sun along the silent shore, thrill with memories of stirring events connected with the lives of my people, and the very dust upon which you now stand responds more lovingly to their footsteps than yours, because it is rich with the blood of our ancestors, and our bare feet are conscious of the sympathetic touch. Our departed braves, fond mothers, glad, happy hearted maidens, and even the little children who lived here and rejoiced for a brief season will love these somber solitudes and, at eventide, they greet shadowy

returning spirits. When the last Red Man shall have perished, the memory of my tribe shall have become a myth, these shores will swarm with the invisible dead of my tribe, and when your children's children think themselves alone in the field or in the silence of the pathless woods they will not be alone. At night, when the cities and villages are silent and you think them deserted, they will throng with the returning hosts that once filled them and still love this beautiful land. Let him be just and deal kindly with my people, for the dead are not powerless. Dead, did I say? There is no death, only a change of worlds."

In July of this year, I received a call from a Native American medical doctor. I had not heard from her in years. She, an elder of the local *Gabrielino-Tongva* (San Gabriel Mission) Tribe, offered to visit since she was in the neighborhood.

"Sure," I said, "I'll be happy to see you again. And wear a feather in your hair when you visit."

She asked me to repeat the last line. When she arrived that evening, she showed me a glass-faced presentation box with a beautiful, huge eagle-feather in it. She told me that, earlier, she had been astonished. "You are psychic! Nobody could have known that I was given this present today by the tribe.

"I know," I told her. "Eagle feathers are religious, to be worn only by the elders." She is now an elder of her tribe.

We are all a bit psychic, some much more than others. This book is a discourse upon our connection with the universe, spirits, and the souls of the people who tread on this sacred ground we call 'The Earth'. We are, indeed, all connected. When you read it, you will be astounded at the ethereal and physical events surrounding ourselves in this universe. Your outlook on life will be vastly improved, and your eyes opened for your own etheric journey through life. Your life will be forever changed.

Chapter One

Electricity Between Soulmates

Ether is the unseen, invisible force or presence in life which has neither mass, density, color, nor other manners of physical measurement. We can measure magnetic power with the Gauss curve, radioactivity by the particles or rays of energy transmitted, black matter in space by assumption, light by photons of energy, yet the invisible ether is still there, unmeasurable everywhere. Religions recognize esoteric principles such as the opening sentences of the Koran saying, *"God is like the Moon in daytime, even though you can't see Him, He is still there."* In the Bible, the wise Son of King David said, *"There is also God in that all streams run to the sea, but the sea is not full; to the place where the streams flow, there they flow again"*. These things can be explained scientifically, but the invisible etheric forces are all around us in a hundred ways which we encounter in many forms. Perhaps, it is better labeled as a true spiritual force or presence. Let us journey through the many etheric-spiritual experiences my clients and I have experienced over the years.

One day, I was having my haircut at a large salon. Because cosmetologists and barbers are great socially verbal creatures, we soon were making small talk, even though I hadn't known her before. Before I left, one

1

of the girls called my attention about another lady in a different open room of the salon.

"Last week," she said, "the girl working over there burned herself with a curling iron." She paused as if something within her was boiling with excitement, egging her to tell me or anybody because it was such a powerful event which had to be shared. "And, I felt her pain and dropped my scissors. I actually felt her pain but seemingly, she didn't feel anything at all."

With that, she waved to her associate, who was coyly smiling at us, and I left with the mysterious event to digest forever.

I never doubted her sincerity because I understand that women are usually socially knit together, more closely than men, but it was an unusual event. On occasion, I still wonder about the miracle of the transmission of pain from one person to another. The only conclusion I have is that they were spiritually bound to each other and shared emotions or events closely enough through the ether that they even shared physical pain together. The burned girl may have been thinking about her friend when the pain impulse was transmitted.

Barbers are very special social people with a knack for conversation and client retention. When I was a child, every Saturday, I would go to the local barber with my father to have my hair mowed while seated on a beautiful, nickel-plated, cast-iron throne with red leather, brass tacked upholstery as I stared down at the Emil J. Koch cast into the footrest. My father would pay for our haircuts, and the barber would give me a new shiny copper penny as a reward for enduring the experience.

As an adult, I would accompany my father to a local barber shop in Malden, Massachusetts. It was a lively place to meet your neighbors and hear the latest rumors. I would see the Mayor who would hold informal office there, mix with the crowd and somehow get a haircut, too. Well, I don't intend to make this a book about barbers, but I believe that such ordinary, wonderful people deserve their time in the limelight.

—⁓—

Many years later, I was preparing a business tax return for Hugo, a general contractor, when he mentioned a fee for a deduction— a fee he paid for a professional barber license. Intrigued, I asked him why a contractor would be maintaining a barber's license. Hugo told me about how hard life was when he was a barber in Hungary after the Russians replaced the Nazis: The 1955 revolution drove many people out of the country and, to place a halt upon the mass migration, the Russians enforced their martial law with tanks. One day, Hugo, a bossy but positive person, schemed to get away. He left all his belongings behind, taking only his scissors and a comb. With his wife, they showed up at the Austrian border where they were stopped by a Russian guard whose priority was to stop people from emigrating from the Communist country.

"Please, I'm just a barber and we are not leaving the country, we are only going on vacation," Hugo the barber told him, pausing only to produce the comb and scissors. "Look, you need a haircut. Let me help you." He took the young soldier's cap off, sat him down in the watchtower, and proceeded to cut his hair.

The soldier liked his haircut and let Hugo through the gate. The barber joined other escapees and later they fled to America. He began as a barber here, and although his later construction business flourished, he never forfeited his barber's license, which had earned him his freedom.

———

There was the wonderful barber who cut the dregs of Humphrey Bogart with a professional dust-off flourish, to establish the ultimate personal service, in the Treasure of Sierra Madre.

———

My friend's father attended Suffolk Law School but never took, or passed, the bar exam in Massachusetts. Instead, he worked as a barber in his own little shop and never practiced law. He did practice with his clients, however, as his jurors, while he worked on their hair personally.

———

Paula S. recounted the story about her father, a young Jewish boy who was sweeping the floor of a neighborhood barbershop after school during the early times of the Second World War, when German soldiers suddenly swooped into the shop and arrested the barbers and customers. The boy was among those herded into the trucks outside.

On the way out of the shop, the officer in charge said, "We need a barber in the company. I think the teenager will do fine. He won't cause us any problems."

With that stroke of luck, the boy sweeper became a barber and was kept out of the concentration extermination camps throughout the war. Later, he married a woman rescued from one of the death camps, and they found their way to America. Sometimes, the Spirit rescues his people in the strangest ways. Spiritual intervention is a miracle when it works.

Cephis maintained a small barbershop in Riverside, California called *The Starlight*. He was in his senior years and by that time, many of his clients had moved away and younger people in the rundown neighborhood were scarce. The little man of color reduced his hours and, eventually, reduced his days while his wife worked as a clerk for the County to pay the bills. His son had gone to college in a southern state. Now, his son was a professor in the same school. I admired both Cephis and his son for becoming an esteemed person from such humble beginnings. Finally, the shop closed, and his wife retired.

One day, his son called. His father had died and he had questions about their little estate. I surprised him when I called him "Doctor" and demonstrated how I knew of him, a medical doctor-professor that his father and I both greatly admired. From then on, it was like talking to an old friend. I always respect medical doctors because it takes a super-human effort and great intelligence to get through the competitive steps and trials to practice medicine. I still remember Cephis, the little barber who helped his son become a big man. America is a blessed nation, and the people are fortunate to accomplish such distant goals. God bless America and its people, especially the common folk like this family.

Fate and luck are part of the etheric spiritual experiences we associate with on a daily basis. People of many cultures reach out to idols or historical figures. It is hard to subscribe to specific reasons for good luck because there is also bad luck. But, sooner or later, we all need help from outside sources beyond our usual knowledge or religious beliefs. Faith covers a lot of ground but is not a true answer. Good intentions, honesty in all dealings, and esoteric spiritual intervention from the unknown are your allies in need. All our souls touch others in different ways. An open heart and mind are helpful on this journey through life. Everybody has different spiritual gifts and our spiritual guides are here to help us use them when needed. Lastly, it is a journey navigated through a sea of people and events, from a barber shop to a crematorium.

Chapter Two

Messages from the Soul

E verybody has dreams. Sometimes, they are significant enough to be remembered. At other times, they portend the future. They could be incomplete and often reflect the past day's struggles, or they could project untenable situations because in a dream, you have no power; you are being pulled along the path of the spiritual ether. Dreams are uncontrollable visits from the ether.

My previous wife, Betty, was from Scotland and, later, England. Our relationship began when I was sidetracked on a flight from Fort Bragg, North Carolina to my new duty station in Germany when the Frankfort landing became fogged in. The flight stopped at Prestwick instead and my buddies and I spent the afternoon at the famous golf course mansion. That evening I visited the little nearby town of Troon where I met Betty and her friend in a coffee shop. Scotland is a cold rugged place occupied by ambitious, tough, honest people. My ancestors, the Bruces, came from the same area of Ayr, but I didn't know of it at the time. I returned a year later to visit and found her working in the Robert Louis Stevenson's bookstore which was run by the elegant granddaughter of the famous author. Later, we would marry, and I would spend my leaves going back and forth across Europe to visit.

Once, in a dream, my wife envisioned a flight. She dreamed of her two aunts, both seated side by side, in an airliner. She had not seen either of them in a long time and her heart leaped with joy, especially since one aunt had passed away years before. She told me about the dream the following morning and was very pleased with seeing them flying together peacefully, in her dream. All she remembered was the ladies seated in front of her on the plane. She wondered why she had dreamed of them but, regardless, it was a pleasant experience to remember her aunties. Later that day, the phone rang; her brother informed her that their aunt had passed away peacefully during the night.

Several years later, she had another dream this time of her father. He was floating in foggy space some distance from her. She reached out for him but he kept floating further away from her. She tried and tried to catch him, but he disappeared into the fog. Then she woke up to find out the next day he passed away that evening. Most people are hesitant to talk about a beloved person visiting to say goodbye when they travel through the ether to make the eternal journey to another life. This is done in the precious out-of-body moments before the silver thread of life breaks. The love between my ex-wife and her aunt was so strong that her aunt traveled through the ether to say that she was joining her sister. The truth is always stranger than fiction. Pleasant memories last a lifetime. I find there are many stories like this left untold, but they are all real events just waiting to be experienced by us again at some future time. Dreams can be very powerful gifts and guides if they are remembered by people with open minds who accept what they see and feel.

Doctor Sherry H. told me that she remembered most of her dreams when she woke. She also possessed immense intuition. One day at a wedding, she told her husband, Andy, that she felt that the bride was hiding something. Andy frowned at the remark and chided her for passing such a judgment on a woman whom she had never met before. Several months later, they learned that the bride's new husband was divorcing her. She had spent over $150,000 worth of cash in that time and was discovered to have had a criminal record and several children out of wedlock.

Still, everyone has their low points and there was a time when this gifted doctor was considering abandoning her profession. During her time as an intern, she had been worn out by relentless demands, fatigued by long hours, and stressed out by the constant assessments by inspecting doctors following every procedure. She was from a family of medical professionals, the fifth to become a doctor, but she seriously considered quitting.

An 18-year-old college student collapsed in the middle of the night. Kevin had been admitted into the hospital the previous day and was treated for a common cold, his condition worsened. Sherry had been the senior resident on duty that night and immediately rushed over. To save him, she needed to immediately insert a breathing tube into his trachea for resuscitation before moving him to the ICU for treatment. Her training and her instructors had told her to place the central line in the jugular or subclavian vein. Her instinct at the time, however, told her otherwise. Sherry realized that she would not have enough time and decided to proceed to violate the protocol by placing a venous catheter into his femoral vein to resuscitate him. Then, she sent him to the ICU. The patient recovered.

The next day, Sherry expected to receive a reprimand from her doctor reviewer for failure to comply with the protocol.

Instead, she received a pat on the back for a job well done. It turned out that the non-standard procedure she used had saved the boy's life. He had been completely misdiagnosed because he was actually suffering from Lemierre's disease and had an infected blood clot in the jugular vein. The normal insertion-of-line procedure would have spread portions of the infected clot all over the boy's body and killed him.

It wasn't happily ever after, however. Kevin was still in critical condition, struggling between life and death in the ICU. His father was given a call regarding his son's condition and in a panic, departed from their home in Hawaii. His mother, who was extremely worried about her son, was at the hospital a few hours before his relapse and collapse. Sherry scrambled to articulate an explanation to the boy's parents to describe what had happened. In her mind, she ran through all of the negative prognosis reports and procedures she had performed. All of which faded the moment she met the boy's mother. Seeing her consuming dread and worry, Sherry realized that she first needed to provide assurance to the anxious mother. She composed herself, looked into the mother's eyes, and said, "I know what you want and I'm going to do it."

From that moment on, Sherry became a part of that family. For a month, like the tube sustaining the boy's life, Sherry sustained the family's sanity. She took great care of Kevin and constantly kept his parents up-to-date on his condition until the boy was able to walk out of the ICU for home. The family always kept in close contact with Sherry afterward. Kevin went on to finish college, married, and is now expecting a baby.

Saving a life is always a cause for celebration. After the incident, Sherry decided to stay the course of becoming a doctor and saving lives. Sherry had reaffirmed her calling by trusting her intuition, which no doubt clearly was spiritual intervention, brought to her over the ether. She violated a protocol which would have cost her a medical career, but sometimes it appears that God Himself is sitting on our shoulders in life or death situations. The gifted professional never hesitates to act outside of the box, like a brave soldier in combat.

Sherry, now an oncologist who sees death in many forms, has her own style of coping with her patients. Her 'Laughter through Healing' gallows-humor notes, based on true events and experiences, are worth quoting:

The patient is a 90-year old man with new skin cancer:

Patient: "I hate to say it, but I don't like young doctors."
Sherry: "Oops."
Patient: "I don't like my surgeon because he is too young."
Sherry: "Oops, again."
Patient: "Young doctors these days are too aggressive."
Sherry: "Okay. I think you need a second opinion with an older doctor. I will try to find the oldest one for you."

And this one with a patient who beat the odds, still living well with stage IV lung cancer after two years.

Patient: "I am not very happy."
Sherry: "Why?"
Patient: "Well, I was told I had six months to live two years ago."
Sherry: "Good, you beat the odds."
Patient: "I got a lot of sympathy back then."
Sherry: "Great, you have a lot of friends."
Patient: "I just spent the last year apologizing to them that I am still here."

As you can see, Sherry has developed her own defense for coping with dying patients. This is one of the gifts this very special person has for her patients.

Debra F. was reading part of this book's manuscript when she paused for a minute, staring past me. Then, she burst into tears. Between sobs, she said, "I've never told anybody about my experience before. My sister-in-law was in the hospital and I was caring for her two young boys. Then, in the middle of one night, I had a dream of her. She asked me to take care of her children and to help them as a foster mother. When I woke up, I was trembling with anxiety. I frantically made phone calls asking about my sister-in-law, but I found out that she had died that evening."

Afterward, Debra took the children in and raised them as her own. They were very well behaved and obeyed her as though she were their real mother. One day, years later, Debra told the boys about the message that she had received from their mother on the evening that she had passed. One of the boys revealed, "Actually, both my brother and I also received a message from Mom that night. She told us that you would be taking care of us from then on, to be good children, and to obey you as good children would."

This was a wonderful event for a passing mother to arrange for the care of her children. Her soul reached out to her loved ones to provide as if she were still there to care for them. God blesses us in many ways.

Deena L., a friend, had a dream in which she met her grandfather. In her dreams, he was dead and walked up to her saying, "Look, I have strong hands." He stood in front of her with his hands outstretched and then faded away. Deena woke up and checked to see if he was okay. He lived in a house on the farm nearby and he was already rising for his daily chores when she knocked on his door. She stayed over coffee to watch the sunrise and worry about what the message was about. Her grandfather had been a school teacher and retired a few years ago. In his time, most people had manual jobs unlike him. He would, however, build furniture in his spare time with his strong hands. Seeing that he was in good spirits, she left him and quit worrying about the message. Three days later, he died while hiking despite apparently being in good health. She interpreted the dream as if he was saying that he too, had strong hands like his parents, even though he only made furniture with them, and did not work on the farm as he would have been. He must have wanted her to know he felt guilty about not doing menial work like his ancestors.

Messages from family members are the strongest messages and are full of meaning and love. They come from powerful spirits which keep us alive for the present and especially the future, not to be ignored or forgotten. They are spiritual messages from the etheric space that we call "Heaven" or the "Holy Spirits".

Chapter Three

A Gift from a Family Psychic

Some occupations physically wear us down and out until we retire. We become slaves to our work and dependent on our paychecks for survival. Other people, mentally exhausted but unable to retire, find minor things to do to 'recharge their batteries', such as watching TV, drinking, or mowing their lawns. Office workers, for example, enter retirement with little to no serious physical injury. However, they often find themselves dealing with much mental wear and tear, suffering from being overweight, high blood pressure, baldness, poor eyesight, computer monitor fixation, and addiction to the evening television, grasping for glimpses of news or programs between endless sonicating commercials.

A client, Ralph, had retired as a construction superintendent many years ago and discovered how to relax for the first time in his life. He was about sixty-years old, had a comfortable union pension, Social Security benefits, and a wife of thirty years. People in management positions like Ralph never leave the job behind. Even when they go home from work, the train barrels along—an endless stream of problems demanding solutions. Over the next few years, he unwound physically and relaxed mentally. After the weight of the work years gradually lifted from Ralph's shoulders, he was a changed person.

One hot sunny day, Ralph won the state lottery. It was a lot of money: six-figures high, with no disclosure until he handed the 1099- form to his tax preparer. The game Ralph played was easy—all you had to do was pick the five winning numbers. The odds were very tough, however. He had luckily, or magically, thought up the correct sequence of numbers. Being a private person, Ralph hid from all subsequent publicity and would not let the lottery people capitalize on advertising his newfound luck. He was a happy fellow and was not bothered by friends or relatives because only his wife and I knew the source of his joy. Out of his winnings, he paid off his mortgage and had money left over.

According to him, he would close his eyes and imagine guessing the five lucky numbers. Until he imagined them, that combination of numbers simply failed to exist. Many people bet using their phone numbers, dates of birth, or addresses, but this was very cold reasoning. Was it possible only because his mind was relaxed—unlabored by taxing job demands, traffic to job sites, and cold dinners when work dragged until late? Could retirement have allowed him to simply put everything out of his mind and see the numbers? Or, maybe, he had a way of gaming the system. Perhaps, there was inside information or collusion. But, he was an honest person. He had done good work all his life and his buildings were still standing. What was his secret? Were there etheric or spiritual influences that brought the numbers to him?

Two years later, he appeared before me with a huge grin.

Oh, no, I thought. He couldn't have been so fortunate a second time. Sure enough, he had won the lottery again for a similar amount. He was a very happy camper with a secret. When we completed his interview, I looked Ralph in the eye. "Nobody on Earth can do this twice in a row, my friend," I told him. "You had some help. Are you psychic?"

He reached over to shake my hand as he answered, "Maybe. I never told anybody, but my mother was psychic. She made a lot of money giving readings and had a very interesting life." The grin was back as he left with his secret.

His spirit had provided his numbers through the ether. After unwinding from his stressful occupation, he had connected with the universe, which had provided the winning formation twice in a row. We are told that stress is a killer, but not that lack of it can make you a clairvoyant winner.

⌒

I know he played the lottery for many years after but never hit the jackpot the third time. He didn't need the money, either. His spirits were satisfied. Maybe communications with the spirits are genetic.

Chapter Four

Unstressed Rewards

Luck is part of life. We hope for it when we play the lottery, push the button on the slot machine or wish for it in a traffic jam. It is such a part of life that some people label their businesess as *Lucky Dry Cleaners* or *The Lucky Restaurant* with the expectation that it will bring clients. The fortune cookie always has a good luck message inside. Asians use *Feng Shui* to orient the doors of their houses and the position of their furniture to the corresponding, auspicious cardinal directions. For those who wish to carry their lucky pieces around, there are lucky rabbits' feet and four-leaf clovers. For the religious folk, there is a great assortment of saints and crosses available. In my family genealogy, a child found a penny on the ground and was noted to have lived a fortuitous life, three-hundred years ago. Sometimes, good luck is mixed or confused with psychic premonition or experiences.

One beautiful sunny Southern California Saturday, I went to a Sheriff's annual auction in Orange County. They were auctioning off property that had been seized from detained criminals. Everything there had been picked over by the officials involved in the handling of County business. There were many briefcases of all sizes from various crimes, and all with broken locks; most badly worn, poor quality rifle cases; broken cameras; shopworn electronic goods; along with a bunch of sundry, Kmart garage-sale material. Among the collection was a box of coins including many wheat pennies worth a cent each and various minor foreign coins. Because it was a beautiful summer morning and I was not in a hurry, I stayed through the auction until they sold me the box of coins for a high bid of $35. I did not expect to find anything valuable in the collection—I didn't have the opportunity to carefully examine because we were not allowed to touch the pile of coins before the auction. I just didn't want to leave empty-handed.

I placed the cigar box in my car and went back to the auction site. From there, I wandered through the nearby county warehouse where discarded and obsolete furniture, electronics, and rusty items resided—awaiting the bid of the scarce collector, lest they be left to an eternity of dust, rust, and obsolescence. That day, they were inviting written bids for everything and, because I was nurturing a fledgling business, I picked through the trash and located many oak tables and some solid chairs. My experience as an auditor of public institutions reminded me that oak tables and chairs were usually cherished possessions because they always looked good and were indestructible. I picked out half a dozen old chairs and tables with little wear and tear showing. As I wrote down the bid for each item I would think, *Everybody will bid $25 for this item so I will bid $26*, and so on. I simply bid a dollar more than I thought other people would bid. That evening, I dumped out the box of coins and found a heavy silver coin emblazoned with Alexander the Great. I looked it up on the computer and found it to be worth at least $1,000.

A month later, I received a call from the Orange County warehouse. The clerk told me to bring a check or cash and pick up the items.

"Which ones did I get?" I asked.

"All of them," he told me. "You bid exactly a dollar more on each. Actually, if you had bid only a penny more, you would still have won them."

I picked up the furniture and, now, had twice as many tables and chairs as I needed for the office. In the end, some of them went home with me. None of the tables ever wore out.

Some days, if the weather is permitting and your mind is open to signals from the beyond, the spirits in the ether can be quite rewarding. If you work long hours, you need to carve time out of your schedule for meditation or exercise to release the many stresses of the day. The daily unwinding should elevate your body and your mind to a better state, on both the plane of health and psychics. A college professor once told me that, in business, one gets so wound up that one loses touch with the world, itself.

"The solution," he said, "is to take a few minutes off, each day and use the time to look outside. Take a break from work to *connect*."

Take a deep breath and connect with the air around you. Connect with the trees, the birds, and the life all around. Connect with the people, with their spirits. Connect with the world. If only just for a few minutes, leave the constricting bomb-shelter that is constantly battered by work and stress. Leave yourself open to the universe, give yourself to the universe, and it will return your openness in kindness. Let your guardian spirits visit.

Chapter Five

Death is Always Nearby

Our primitive ancestors worshiped the hand of ethereal spirits in the thunderous cry of lightning streaking across the sky. The immense power would strike fear into their hearts as the power and fury of the bolt of energy from the sky could only have been induced by a god— an angry one.

When I was a child, lightning struck a large tree in front of a home only two doors away from us. The strike split the tree in two and one of the halves fell upon the roof of the nearby house. The other half remained rooted to the ground and inch-by-inch, its bark would slowly encompass its wounded side, over the subsequent years. This was a wonderfully exciting event for all the children in my neighborhood with the woeful exception of my friends in the house with the smashed roof.

Two decades following the strike and three gruesome years in the Army, I had a night job delivering booze for a liquor store in Malden, Massachusetts. In those days, these stores were called "package goods stores" because it was sinful to be seen with liquor, so you bought a "package" with booze in it. The job paid minimum wage plus tips which helped me save money later to attend Northeastern University in the evenings. My regular sales job paid little, and I had a family to support. The military offered no educational benefits and I was on my own financially.

One evening, it was raining cats and dogs as I loaded the back of the store's old Chrysler. The aged car had a huge trunk for the task and an interesting push-button for an electronic shifting automatic transmission. There were times when I would start the car and push the button just to listen to the whirr underneath and resounding clunk as the electric motors moved gears somehow into 'Reverse' or into 'Drive'. Then, I would be off to the boonies in Saugus, the dry town nearby, to tour the motels and homes which had called in their orders.

This evening was particularly dark with the rain driven by gale winds, accompanied by flashes of lightning and booming thunder from off in the distance. I arrived at a remote hill in Saugus and parked near the front of an old house flanked by a huge elm tree on either side of its walkway. In New England, elm trees are planted everywhere, growing tall and gracefully gigantic—the Sequoias of the East. I delivered the goods and was paid with a small tip, stuffing it into my pocket as I walked past the trees. Suddenly, there was a huge, overpowering flash of light and an encompassing explosion; then, nothing but darkness.

When I woke, I found myself laying on the ground, covered by a pile of blackened tree branches. It took me a long, dazed minute to realize that one of the elm trees had been struck by lightning and its remains had fallen all over and around me. I was neither hurt nor injured, only dazed by the circumstances. I had no idea how long I had been unconscious. I extricated myself and climbed out of the mountain of branches. After that struggle, I began lumbering back towards the Chrysler. Along the way, I noticed electric lines sparking on the ground and skirted away from them. Rain was still pouring into the darkness.

A police officer was in the middle of the street, directing traffic away from the downed tree, the debris of which extended into the street. He spotted me and, as if I had been curiously exploring the site, hollered at me, "Hey kid, get the hell out of there!"

He had no idea that I had been struck by lightning while the tree took the hit on top of me. I found the car untouched and drove off to tell my tale to the store manager and, later, to Betty, my wife.

On the journey home, I made note of the time and slowly came to grasp that a long time must have passed between the strike and when the cops arrived. I wondered how long the officer had been there. I had no idea how long I had been out but began to realize how lucky I had been to have not been grievously hurt or killed. I did not experience any burns, bruises, bumps, or injuries. The odds of surviving a direct or indirect lightning strike are exceptionally minuscule. Afterward, I reflected that the hand of God or his appointed guardian must have spared me. Help from the ether had also saved me many times from death, before and afterward. Though I admit that some of my crossings with harm's way may have been deliberate. It seems I have always been on the path of danger and my spirits were there constantly to save me. Some would call it luck, but I believe the term for this event is "miraculous intervention".

In 2017, it was reported that an entire herd of unfortunate reindeer was struck and killed by lightning in a clearing in Finland. This was a terrible form of lightning which does not strike directly from the sky but, after descending, moves from one position over the ground to another.

Recently, a client named David M. told me about an incident where he, as a teen, was walking in the woods near his home in Idaho during a lightning storm. A bolt of lightning tore out of the woods beside him and thundered past in a blast of noise and light. It snaked over the ground and left a char mark in the dirt before disappearing, completely missing David. He ran home terrified and for a few minutes, he was speechless—unable to talk to his parents. He had been saved by divine intervention, as so many others have.

These are the experiences that enrich life and fill every person with uniquity. Until David learned of my own experience with lightning, he had opted never to tell anybody about his own encounter. He was blessed and when you get to know this fellow, you will find a wonderful passionate soul connecting him with his wife and children. I believe there is always a special reason for people to be spared the bolt of death.

Chapter Six

Gifts from the Common Folk

All things are tied and blended together in the ether. People feel things, see things, experience things, and live with these experiences and events that other people cannot be weighed, measured, or seen. Everybody has experienced a déjà vu encounter with a stranger who has seemed familiar. Perhaps those are past life encounters. There are times when strangers look at you and break out in a big smile as if you were a long-lost friend. We could all be from many times and places. Life is a continuous process and we occupy time and space almost forever on this Earth.

I once had a client named Janet. She was a very ordinary person whose husband was a roofer—a very dangerous profession. What is interesting is that this young woman disclosed a unique relationship she had with the Universe. She told me that she had a special gift: she could see halos around people.

I know much has been written about auras which are supposed to encapsulate our physical being and are supposed to be visible as a glowing, pale, light emanating from all living beings. But here was a simple person who was seeing halos around the heads of other people. She said the halos were of different colors. Looking at me, she noted that mine was a light-blue and commented that some people's halos were bad news. She told me, "When I see a black halo on a person, I walk on the other side of the street to keep away from his bad spirit."

How amazing that a person could detect the quality of the spirit in you by the color of your halo. This person had a great fear of bad spirits and believed that her guardians were always nearby to comfort and protect her.

The Catholic people of the Philippines, Filipinos, all have at least one Last Supper carving or painting in their kitchens. Because I love wood carvings, there is one in my kitchen. Most have silver halos around the Apostles and Christ's halo is always golden. If artists, with their enlightened sensuality, and other truly religious people with higher levels of spirituality could see these characteristics, it would only be natural that common folk, with an enlightened spirit, would also be able to see and feel the gifts given by the ether. Maybe there is a black halo around some of the people you try to avoid because they make you uncomfortable.

Have you ever looked into the eyes of a murderer? I have. There are two kinds. One is the person whose eyes are filled with the unquenchable flames of rage, the sheer intensity of their anger disconnecting them from the rest of us. The other is the cold-blooded figure devoid of a soul. The latter looks like a human, moves like a human, talks like a human. But, when you look into their eyes, you won't be able to find the glint of humanity. That light has been lost to them, leaving nothing but an abyss hungering for the light of others—a black hole, preying upon the light of the stars.

Hopefully, you will encounter or have already encountered some silver or golden halos with the rare, truly charismatic people who give their all for us. They are out there, waiting for us to find them in the ether of our existence. Only a few of us will see their halos, beckoning from afar.

Another client in our journey through life is a hairdresser. Diane H., like most of us, is a very ordinary lady with an ordinary job (remember what I said about barbers?). No, she is not preaching before you in the church, nor is she being interviewed on television. But, like Janet who could see halos, she also has the gift and quite clairvoyant.

Diane sees auras around people in a sophisticated way. She sees them as a shadowy form hanging beside the person she is watching. This life force floats around the person; behind, near, to the side, or in front of the person. She and her husband both have brilliant, silver auras. They are truly a beautiful couple. She feels her own auras and is aware of her gift. The auras this lady sees turn gray with time, changing as the person ages and acquires wisdom. Dark auras encroach upon outside presences. Black auras make her uncomfortable. Diane told me that my aura is brilliant blue, streaked with gray because I am highly analytical. According to her, a silver aura is the finest aura, and that the Last Supper figure of Christ has a silver aura.

Neither the halo lady nor the aura lady sees green, red, or purple associated with anybody. Not all colors are present in their spiritual spectrum. These are amazing gifts from people we bump into on the freeways of life.

Now, you know why some people smile when they see you while others look through you. Blame it on the body chemistry that creates auras or halos with your soul, if not a past life association.

Chapter Seven

Meeting a Sister in Heaven

Tony was middle-aged with greying hair and extra weight. He was a mildly-tempered person originating from the Midwest and had just sold off the out of state family farm. A client of many years, he would discuss personal affairs whenever he visited. My occupation has made me a good listener and I discovered, long ago, that the other side of empathy was to encourage the client to communicate because we all need someone to talk to. Clients are at ease with me and our souls are on the line when they come into my office.

He never mentioned his marriage which I never asked, but he did mention about his pre-teen children—a young son and an older daughter who he supported alone. On one visit, he mentioned that his daughter had passed away from a tragic combination of genetic matching between him and his wife. He described how the debilitating disease affected her growth and slowly but ultimately, caused her death. She was only eleven at the time. A life unfulfilled. Only a year older than her brother.

Now, his son was bound to the same fate. It must have been awful for the father to know that both children would pass away at such an early age. Children of these ages are always close together and the son would still be grieving the loss of his sister when it was his turn to go to the hospital.

The entire time we spoke about his tax situation, the father had tears in his eyes. He broke down afterward and told me of the little boy's last days in the hospital. Many clients tell me I am like a father to them when they ask for advice, but this time, I could only listen and allow the tears to flow.

For years, the boy had known death was coming. When his sister died, he could not understand why she had to give up her life at such a young age. Perhaps, it had been easier for his father to comprehend, because we become more experienced and exposed to tragedy while building immunities as we grow older. But now the client sobbed, his voice and face changing, betraying his vulnerabilities.

The terrible event unfolded in the hospital room as the boy labored to stay alive. The nurses helped but could not hold back their remorse for the child who struggled with all his heart to cling to life but was doomed, nonetheless. The days dragged on and the little boy refused to submit to the Grim Reaper, even as his strength diminished. His struggles were in vain, though, and the inevitable relentlessly encroached upon his besieged body.

Finally, the father held his dying son in his arms. He felt it was time for his boy to let go of the suffering. "Son," he whispered in his child's ear, "you must let go now and join your sister. She is waiting for you in heaven." He paused to study his son's weary eyes before repeating his words.

There was a minute of silence as the little boy absorbed the message. Then, he looked up at his father and, as he smiled, his face relaxed. The stress—the pain of a year's endeavor—left his body and his soul went to join his soulmate. The father was suddenly alone in tears, mourning his children.

Once, as a young manager for a multinational company, I was sent to a consultant psychologist for a full day's battery of ability and personality tests. The exams concluded that I was unusually bright but lacked empathy for other people. I was ambitious, and it showed. After listening to my client on this day and learning about the connection between the children's souls, I had enough empathy for a lifetime. Now, the children could continue their lives in heaven. Life is full of dark times and they change us forever, in one way or another.

Chapter Eight

Hydrophobic

As a child, I was always short of breath because of severe asthma. Like my big Labrador dog, wary of anything that might get between him and his chow, I was wary of water due to my breathing problems. This wariness solidified after my mother took me to the YMCA for a swimming lesson when I was a small boy. The instructor lined up all the boys on the edge of the pool and tossed us, one by one, into the water. Some swam out. I was one of the others and needed to be rescued. From that time on, I had been afraid of water because I knew I couldn't swim.

Years later, my mother took me and my little brother to the Revere Beach in Massachusetts. The beach was gently sloped with low wave action except when the nor'easter storms visited the Atlantic. There was a huge 25-foot-high seawall for those occasions.

On that sunny hot summer day, I decided to overcome my fear of water. I spotted a piece of wood floating well out into the bay and resolved to walk out and bring it back, no matter how far out it was.

Hence, I waded into the water and headed towards the little wooden object bobbing on the small waves. As I waded further, the waves diminished and evened out considerably. I kept walking on my toes until the ocean was up to my chin, trying to keep my head above water. The tidal currents began to lift my feet off the sand below. I was on my tiptoes when I finally grasped the little stick and began heading back, fearful that the tide would pull me out with it. I slowly made it back to my mother's blanket where she slept and wondered if I might have drowned. My mother had noticed neither my absence nor my trip into the sea.

Many years later, I was doing my basic military training duty at Fort Dix, New Jersey. Some went into the military as a volunteer or through conscription. I met many nice people of my age at 18 and many older college student draftees who were able to serve only six months with extended active reserves instead of the two-year draft. Basic training would turn out to be the best time of my three-year enlistment and I made many new friends. I tailored my fatigues and became gung-ho, actually enjoying the military. One good experience was when I shot "expert" with the M-1 rifle at 300 yards and received a three-day pass. Keeping a high-powered Winchester Model 70 rifle of the same caliber at home proved an advantage.

This led me to visit a newfound friend, a P.E. high-school teacher named Karl from the Grand Concourse of the Bronx in New York City, over the next weekend. His wife's younger sister, Delores, was also there and we both had a wonderful weekend visiting the Empire State Building and the Salt Water Deep Pool in Coney Island, one of a strip of entertainment events along the beach boardwalk. Since Delores was an excellent swimmer, she decided to teach me how to swim at the pool. We went into the water with her holding on to me. The pool was ten feet deep, for experienced swimmers only.

I managed to thrash around in the water for a few moments before sinking like a rock. At the time, I was in perfect physical shape—my asthma had left me the year before. Still, I was heavier than the salt water and settled on the bottom of the pool. I held my breath as I attempted to leap to the surface. The leap was an effort in vain. At the peak of my ascent, there was still at least four feet of water overhead. Then, I sank.

The seconds began to feel like minutes; then hours, then an eternity as my oxygen faded. I prepared myself to take a deep breath of water that would kill me. Then, a lifeguard came out of nowhere, plucked me off the bottom, and took me to the poolside with a perfect backhand stroke. He saved my life. As he deposited me on the concrete, he was surprised to see me rise and stand up in front of him and the anxious crowd of onlookers. I thanked him profusely for saving my life, then left with Delores. The lifeguard had a totally astonished look on his face, shocked that the man he saved simply got up and walked away without needing further attention. I hope his employers gave him a medal or accommodation afterward for performing such a rescue.

As a child, I had many life-threatening situations. My mother would rush me, blue in the face, to the hospital during severe asthma attacks. It was all about breathing.

In another incident, a jack slipped from under a car that I was working on. The mechanic and I were exchanging a wrecked junkyard differential on my old 1949 Cadillac and I had just moved my head from under the frame. Without warning, the jack slipped sideways on the new, soft driveway asphalt. The heavy car crashed, crushing the wooden boxes my mechanic had placed under the frame. I was left in utter shock, having only narrowly survived the accident. I was sixteen, at the time.

Years before, I had been firing an old .22-caliber derringer in the cellar at home when a round ricocheted back through my hair. That was my last day shooting inside the house.

Even after my family moved to Malden, Massachusetts and up to this day, I feel a deep connection to my old town of Saugus. While I was in high school there, my mother found me an after-school job at a new A&P supermarket on the turnpike. It was a nice job, but it was out of the way. Every day, I would have to take two buses and walk a bit to get there. The store had a nice feature of putting everybody's groceries in a fiberglass box and sending it on rollers through the wall where I would place them in the cars as the people drove up. I loved the job and clients and the weather was usually quite pleasant.

However, one winter day, it was snowing heavily when I got to work. I was wearing a heavy woolen coat left over from the First World War and was prepared for the weather. As the snow, wind, and cold grew heavier with the encroaching nighttime, I was glad when the store manager decided to close early. By this time, the customers had been calling the storm "a blizzard" and fierce winds seemed intent on living up to that title. Snow buffeted the bus's windshield, quickly piling on the wipers and obscuring the driver's vision. The bus stopped at Cliftondale Square, ten miles from where I was going, and everybody got off.

"We are shutting down because of the weather," the driver announced. Then, without another word, he drove out of sight.

I was desperate and panicked because there were no other vehicles on the road and all the businesses were shut down except for a drugstore. I ran into the drugstore and called a neighbor on the payphone. They offered to take me in for the night if I could get there. They lived almost a mile away, downwind. The drugstore closed behind me as I headed for my old neighborhood.

That walk was the longest of my life. I bucked the winds and plodded through the sidewalk drifts as they got higher and higher. Many years before, I had walked the same route although there was no visibility, so, I knew the way. An hour later, I arrived at their familiar house, which was three doors down the street from my family's old residence, and was welcomed by my lifetime friend, Richard. His family insisted that I take a bath to warm up and thaw out. I must have looked like Zhivago after his escape in the Siberian winter, a frozen snowman arriving from a death walk. It ended as a wonderful evening with friends, but I had always wondered what would have happened if I didn't have their phone number or any other place to go. Later, Richard would be the godfather of my first child, who bears his name. I remember his fine home as the home the elm tree struck when half of it took out their porch and roof in the lightning storm.

My luck was still holding. My guardian spirits were there in the ether to give me their support when I needed them most. The spiritual forces were at work on that day, many times before and afterward. Again, like the tree crashing on me, I was able to walk away unscathed every time. My Guardian, the unseen keeper of my etheric space, was always there to give me another chance. I would need him many times again because, afterward, I signed up for the paratroops.

Chapter Nine

Silver Thread of Life

Margaret was a single nurse, of about thirty years of age. She never wore a uniform except at work and she was usually quiet and businesslike—never prone to shop-talk, even when she came in for her annual appointment. One day, she called about a tax matter and we ended up talking for an hour. As usual, she was very professional but, this time, she was open to discussion. We all have things we wish to share, and I suppose that on that occasion, Margaret was eager to share something. She had had a near-death experience. I don't know why people tell me their private hidden stories, but I am always a good listener when they begin. Maybe they pick up my interest in them and the esoteric events of everybody's existence. Call it sensitivity.

In the previous year, Margaret had gone into the hospital for her own surgery to remove her appendix—a fairly common procedure. Common or not, however, every surgery carries some inherent risk. A misjudgment of the anesthesia, a slip of the hand, an accidental puncture to an artery and suddenly a life is snuffed out. Margaret died on the operating room table that day.

She found herself in a tunnel leading to God. Dancing flickers of light illuminated a path blanketed by an aesthetic brilliant array of flowers. Music filled the comfortably warm air, soothing her soul and beckoning her toward liberation from all pain. However, by way of a sudden miraculous turnaround, she was revived and woke with the doctors and anesthesiologist hovering over her body. I don't know if she was presented with a question by God about going away or returning as many people relate. She told me that her life changed afterward. She appreciated her earthly existence much more after returning from the brink of death. As a nurse, she also saw a higher value in working with the elderly and their medical problems.

Things had been different starting from almost a year later. One day, she was around when a patient died, nothing she wasn't accustomed to. As the lady passed, the nurse's attention was captured by a silver thread that left the patient's body and faded into the ceiling. She looked at the doctors who were present, but they simply looked away. The doctors, who already had witnessed it before, didn't want to talk about it.

Over the course of the next year, she saw the silver thread again and, always, the silver thread of the patient's soul would leave their body and fade into the room overhead. The doctors would look at each other but never say a word. It was a medical fact which was not in the textbooks or discussed outside of the operating room. Time and time again, she saw the silver thread of the patient's souls, their energy force, leaving them. Medical specialists and scientists like to talk about measurable provable scientific facts but this one doesn't fit any textbook. Sensitive people like Margaret are like magnets of the soul and they become aware of many things us common folk are not aware of. They are very special people.

It fits the Bible, however. The soul is real and not to be measured or weighed in earthly terms. The rabbi Ecclesiastes was aware of the silver thread when he said, *"The silver cord is snapped, and the spirit returns to God who gave it"*. Only the gifted and chosen are able to see it and recognize the esoteric substance. How could you have Karma or after-life without a soul? And how could you have a soul without your silver thread of life? To take the discussion a step further, many British and Scandinavians have an old custom of opening a window when a person dies, to let the soul out.

It is also believed by many that the soul is connected to the earthly material body, but that it is connected to the physical being by the silver thread. This allows the soul to travel as in Margaret's near-death experience to other places. It also occurs in out-of-body experiences, allowing the soul to look down on the person with cool disconnection. When a person dies, that thread is broken and returns the soul to heaven via the ether.

I heard a story from a client about his friend who was declared dead from a massive heart attack in a shopping area parking lot. Later, at the hospital operating room, he experienced a near-death encounter. He looked down at the doctors and nurses on his return and saw halos or auras around each of them before he returned to Earth. The soul is an amazing force in the lives of people who are exposed to the ether. I personally believe the good people are returned to live out their lives, the bad guys go away. God has blessed the people who return.

Chapter Ten

The Fateful Breath

John was a 30-year old professional physical therapist. He was very reserved and guarded while his wife was much more sociable. In line with his work, he kept himself in great physical shape. At some point in our conversation, his wife mentioned that John had previously worked for years as a paramedic with an independent ambulance service until his life changed forever.

"He had to change professions," his wife began. Her hands clasped his, tightly and lovingly. "He was having terrible problems with his health. Couldn't sleep nights, incredibly stressed, physically uncomfortable all the time."

From there, John decided to take over the conversation. "Before the incident, I used to love my work. I love helping people, saving them from whatever situation I could as a first responder. My unit would have lots of time on our hands to exercise and read between calls but, when the dispatcher called out, our adrenaline shot up and we rushed to the accident or home to save a life. Then came the incident that changed my life."

"We had a house call for an elderly male who was lying on the floor of his house. He had a very low pulse and was having trouble breathing.

He stopped breathing after we arrived. I responded with CPR and began working on his chest coupled with mouth-to-mouth resuscitation. He showed some signs of response as I worked on him, but it didn't hold. He quit responding and his life signs faded away for good."

"Suddenly, I felt something horrible; his dying breath taking over my whole body like I was going to die. For a few minutes, I was helpless, unable to do anything but sit next to him as his body cooled down. Finally, my partner pulled me up and I let out a scream, 'Take me out of here!' My partner-driver led me away while calling the dispatcher for more help. I was so incapacitated that I was unable to get the old man's body into the gurney and ambulance."

"For months afterward, I would have nightmares that would drag uncontrollable discomfort and depression into my waking hours. It was the darkest time of my life. I held back on responses and couldn't do my job afterward, fearful of what could happen again. I tried to get disability but finally gave my notice instead. I went back to school for physical therapy and tried to get back into shape. The effects are still with me but not as bad as before. Now, I am functioning on a higher level. It still bothers me and I have negative moments thinking about what happened. Like PTSD, it haunts me."

<hr />

This innocent man had inhaled the dying breath of a stranger and it had changed his life and profession forever. Possibly, John had shared in the deceased's horrific descent into the dark void of hell. Doctor Elisabeth Kubler Ross, who studied dying people, briefly wrote about the abyss into which some people fall. Christianity and some other religions call it "Hell". Life-changing events are unpredictable in the etheric world and can sometimes be irrevocable and meaningless. Having a good, honest life and soul can be the saving grace in times of unexpected danger. Having a guardian angel is even better.

Chapter Eleven

Restless Teenager

When my family moved to Malden, Massachusetts, I was enrolled in the fifth grade of the local school system. I soon found out that I could read on my own and would rapidly finish the books in the reading class while the other kids plodded aloud through the text, word by tedious word. Since I always finished on my own, I would be out of place when it became my turn to read out loud and because of that, I would be sentenced to stand in the corner after class as punishment. My mastery of the "Reinhart Writing System" was poor—probably because my asthma bothered me every day—and for that, I was sentenced to stay after class even longer to practice more of my terrible handwriting.

During that time, my father offered me a 25-cent weekly allowance, which didn't go very far. I was fortunate enough to find a local paper route for afternoon and Sunday delivery. The Sunday route was a struggle because the weekend papers were very heavy, and my route had a big hill. To deal with this, I built wagons from the axles and wheels of flimsy baby-carriages. Thus, while most people were in a church or a synagogue, I would spend my Sunday mornings pulling my makeshift wagons up and down the street of Franklin Avenue. I was paid a penny a paper for the dailies and three cents for the Sundays. The take, including tips, was about $13 weekly—a third of the minimum wage, at the time. I bought a change dispenser machine which hooked on my belt and after the Sunday delivery, when everybody was up and back from Church, I would return for payments. I paid for my own clothes and was from then on, independent. When my asthma bothered me too much or when it was snowing, I would hire a kid from the neighborhood to push the wagon up the hill for me.

Several years later, I bought a ChemCraft set with which I performed a few harmless experiments. Since I enjoyed the experience a lot, I decided a week later to go big on chemistry and took over the cellar room at home. I visited the two drug stores in nearby Suffolk Square and ordered laboratory supplies and chemicals (chemically pure, if available, and more expensive reagents, if not). I was able to order almost anything and signed the poison book when I picked up the goods. Whenever I wasn't reading Isaac Asimov science fiction, I was reading everything I could find on chemistry. My mother had a single, large, *Lincoln Library* encyclopedia at home and there was a local junior-high-school library where I went to school. Later, I was bounced from the main library across from the high school because I wasn't old enough. During that time, I had amassed thousands of dollars' worth of chemicals. A huge Mendeleev periodic chart with atomic weights and electron valances hung from the ceiling, so I could mix my chemicals on a metric scale by the mole. I tested every chemical reaction, common explosive, and reactive compound known. I even had fuming nitric and concentrated sulfuric acid to make nitroglycerin, but I ultimately held off because it would be too sensitive to handle and probably would have heat cooling problems from the acids mixing with the glycerol. It could also have easily blown me and the house up. Testing it would be a problem because it was so powerful and dangerous.

Somehow, my knowledge of chemistry advanced beyond what I could read. I was able to compute things without formulas. Nitrous oxide was one such example. This strange explosive is composed of metallic iodine which is nitrated. I simply took household ammonia water and quickly immersed iodine that I had ground from crystals and left on filter paper overnight. Iodine is a strange element which evaporates from the solid form if left in the open. Leave a crystal on a paper and it will disappear. It made a strange, highly sensitive explosive which would leave a purple spot when it exploded.

I installed a fan in the window and wired it so that it would suck fumes out of the room whenever I flicked the lights on. One of my creations was a highly explosive powder of magnesium and potassium chlorate, similar to the material used in military hand grenades. Once, this almost blew my right hand off and took some of my hearing away. I had surgery on my hand and my ears rang for three days. Upon reflecting, I felt sorry for my innocent family when I reduced potassium bromide to pure, deep-red bromine liquid. Some of the noxious fumes escaped from the retort causing my family to have sleeping problems that evening. I was a terrible son, but my parents left me alone. They had no idea or understanding of what I was doing in the basement.

There were two other events worth mentioning. The first was a self-made, paper-wrapped, zinc and sulfur rocket. I set it up in the backyard on a stormy night while everyone else was reading the newspaper or watching Ed Sullivan. I lit the paper rocket and stood back as a huge, flickering green flame emerged, lifting my creation a yard off the ground. For a full minute the flame licked at the ground as the rocket hovered, suspended in the air. Then it exploded with a deafening roar and huge green flash that rattled the windows of the house. A moment later, my father tore out of the house cursing and chased me down the hill. I escaped and kept out of sight for the rest of the week. The neighbors thought it was lightning, so nobody called the cops.

Then, there was the time when I put together a blockbuster with several ounces of my super explosive. It was about the size of a shotgun shell and I knew that I needed a secluded place to fire it off. I took the bus to Saugus and walked around the Cliftondale Hill until I connected with the dirt road that entered the marsh that stretched out for miles. It was dusk, and I walked a half-hour into the desolate place with no houses, street lights, or activity. The road went directly into the tidal marsh but stopped at a huge rock, where people would go target shooting. This was a perfectly isolated place to fire off my firecracker with a full mile between the rock and the hill with the town far on the other side. I set it on the side of the rock, lit the fuse, and ducked for cover. Moments later, it exploded with a brilliant white flash and huge boom which reverberated as a shock wave that spread towards the hill before rolling back. The amount of energy expended was incredible and I stood, staring in awe—just as a set of headlights started down the road over a mile away. Trembling with excitement and anxiety, I hid in the weeds as a police car rumbled down the road. It stopped at the rock, its searchlights sweeping both sides of the road. They pointed into the brush where I was hiding but didn't see me. I was fortunate to escape and decided to never again fire off such a device. But not before I tested an underwater version.

In my junior year of high school, I let the paper route go and began drifting. I went to MIT for a free lunch with the desire to become a scientist but found myself trudging through general classes preparing me to work in gas stations or whatever was out there. I avoided the library across the street because I was unwelcomed.

College just wasn't for me and that coincided with my family background; my parents were almost illiterate, a product of the Nova Scotia backwoods where my father had quit school at ten to support his family after his father had died. Because he became a master tool- and-die-maker he could read a blueprint better than a newspaper.

I bought an old car and, every week, I would complain to the school nurse that my asthma was bothering me so that she would let me go for the day. Then, I would take my fine Winchester Model 70 high-powered rifle and go target shooting in the Saugus Woods or in back of the pond.

One day, a man from the State Department of Rehabilitation interviewed me. The interview started off well enough but, when the topic of my history with asthma was broached, the man suddenly became very interested in ensuring that I would not become as a ward of the State. He arranged for a full battery of examinations for ability and other traits, so he would know what he should do with me. A week after the full day of exams, we met again. He was amazed by the results and offered me a full scholarship to any college in the country. They would pay for everything. I had merely to apply and qualify.

I had not seen a counselor since my last attendance in school and didn't know what to do. I went home and informed my parents who offered no advice. The last my father had seen of a classroom was in Nova Scotia; because he was left-handed they tried to force him to use his right hand for everything, because he was a leftie. I felt as though I was in the wrong school program and nobody could offer any guidance for me. I passed on the offer and continued drifting. Finally, after another year of English Language dissection, my most hated subject, I graduated.

A year later, I took a simple AFQT test for enlistment with the Army. Though it would return years later, at the time it seemed although my asthma had left. I scored 96 out of 99 possible points and they offered me entry to all the military schools. I elected explosives ordnance demolition, my favorite subject. I would wear a bomb patch on my shoulder and receive combat pay in peacetime—after a physical in Boston. This time, I lied about my history of asthma and they sent me to Fort Dix, New Jersey on a train.

That was the beginning of my flight from my home and my family. Everything was left behind. A free spirit was released to the world— right into the jaws of the military. The Army owned me which I welcomed at first. Later, I realized it was cursed. What you see is not what you get. Fortunately, I had my spirits guarding me, as they had always done. My spirit guardians would serve me well in my new occupation.

Chapter Twelve

Out of Body Fireman

The fireman was a tall, solidly-built individual. Of Anglo-Saxon descent, Gerry A. was very independent and always had his feet on the ground financially. Over the years, he had physically tired of his profession and after the Rodney King riots in Los Angeles, and the subsequent riot training added to firemen's regimen, he began considering retirement. I always respected him because he had the courage and strength to combat fires. We would discuss politics and he would always berate his union and work politics.

One day, he told me about the terrifying experiences that he had dealt with as a child. After falling asleep at night, his soul would leave his body and he would find himself looking down at his sleeping body. Then his soul would go through the ceiling, through the attic, and then through the roof. He would find himself outside, looking down at his house, at the treetops in the yard, and at the neighborhood. It was a strange, unnerving experience. After a few minutes, he would return to his body and bolt awake, sweating profusely.

These episodes occurred so frequently that he began to fear going to sleep at night. He never knew when it would happen and didn't understand why it happened. He had no control of his movements during these occurrences. He was afraid to tell anybody because they would think he had made them up or that he was missing some hardware in his head. After more voyages over the neighborhood, he developed an intense fear that his soul would soon leave him and not return.

Finally, after a bad night, afraid to go back to sleep, he recognized that something had to be done. He approached his mother who could be a very calm person when he needed help, as a last resort. She calmly told him to say the Lord's Prayer when he went to bed. She assured him that the Lord would take care of the problem. That evening he said his prayers and slept soundly. For weeks afterward, he would experience anxiety when he went to bed but, after saying his prayers, he was able to sleep soundly without the flight of his soul. The out of body experiences never returned and the client still says his prayers.

Sometimes the soul is searching for something in the ether that we don't understand, something that his mother understood clearly. It appears that our fate is always in the hands of the Lord. As it is said, keep the faith and good things will come to you.

Chapter Thirteen

The Demon

This is the only story that I have recorded where the source was not a client. In less developed countries, ethereal occurrences are very real; even commonplace. People living out in the country or on the outskirts of urban areas all have their own recounts of personal encounters or of close relatives and friends who have encountered unnatural spirits and demons. Entire communities and cultures are immersed in the ethereal. People fear curses and superstitions and the great unknown. This brings us to some missionaries who encountered dark spirits, recently in the hot humid isolated Southern Mexico jungles.

This priest spent two years in Mexico as a Mormon missionary, bringing his faith to the local remote villages. Peter loved his work and didn't believe in black spirits, believing they were mostly hallucinations from people on drugs or superstitions carried around by ignorant, isolated people. His beliefs took a sharp turn when he had his own terrifying experience.

Peter had been making his way through one of the poorer, less populated regions, bringing his church's Word to people's doorsteps.

One day, on his last visit before turning in for the night, he met the usual kind but disinterested response. He thanked the family and prepared to leave but noticed a brief pause of silence and an exchange of glances amongst the family. After reaching some manner of hushed consensus, they told the missionary about their distant neighbor, a woman living a kilometer away who had been widowed a few years ago and had never been the same since. The family told the missionary that they were concerned about the widow who they said had demonstrated suicidal tendencies and asked the missionary to investigate into the matter for them. The missionary gladly agreed to visit and spread the word of the Lord to the direly needy widow.

Unfortunately, Peter and his missionary brothers quickly became overwhelmed with other duties and the task of visiting the widow fell to the side, all forgotten. In the end, another missionary agreed to visit poor woman.

Weeks later, Peter took a taxi on his way back to the mission returning from a marriage counseling session. Along the way, the ringing of his phone roused him from his reminiscing and he picked it up.

It was the missionary who went to visit the widow with another assistant. There was panicked screaming between breaths; the missionary told him they were on the run and needed immediate help.

Fearing that a local drug lord was chasing them, Peter hurriedly asked where they were and learned that they were running to the mission. He convinced the taxi driver to turn the car around. They raced off in the direction of the two fleeing missionaries and found them running at breakneck speed towards the mission. The taxi stopped, and Peter opened the doors calling out to his companions.

The missionaries jumped in just as the car sped away. Peter glanced back to see a horrifying, shadowy, large, pseudo-human apparition disappearing from the corner of the road behind them as they turned away.

The two missionaries were rendered speechless and fidgeted with their fingers constantly while glancing behind them.

It wasn't until the next day before Peter was able to get the details from them. They explained that when they visited the widow's place, she had covered the place with archaic markings and incomprehensible satanic signs. The small cottage was lit only by candlelight and there were many objects lying around that they were unable to identify. Regardless, the woman seemed harmless and somewhat troubled so they attempted to tell her about the Word of Christ. She remained silent the majority of the time, only breaking her silence to muse about how she had already been saved and that her husband had never left her.

The missionaries hadn't felt as though they were successfully communicating and were confused at her stoic lack of attention. Not knowing how to further help, they decided to leave things as they were and rose to give her a blessing—perhaps they would return some other time.

As they raised their hands in her direction, she returned to her deathly silence. Wondering if it was working, they continued the blessing; suddenly, she abruptly dropped to the floor. Worried, they rushed towards her slack form, only to be met with sharp growls from her as she contorted with her stance misshaped. Then, she charged towards them and they ran for their lives.

There are things we encounter in life which are better left unanswered and certainly avoided at all costs. Not all things are good in the ether of our existence. Black forces do exist for some of us. Apparitions certainly exist for some people caught up in the ether of purgatory and Hell.

There are things we don't want to know about life which are best left unexplained.

At this time, I wish to point out a terrifying experience from my military days in Germany. Sometimes, *we* are our own worst demons. The remainder of the chapter focuses on self-inflicted desolation by mankind—evil people manipulating and corrupting the spirits of others. The Weimar Republic of Germany was born of the economic catastrophe resulting from the burden of repaying of World War I debts to the Allies. It was a free-wheeling society recently liberated from war and economic calamity. It was the late-1920s and everybody was happy the bad times were over, sort of like America in the current period. Then the Depression struck. The Fascist Nazi government rose to power, promising good times again, and the Second World War was on. History always repeats itself and in 1960 our airborne combat unit was sent to the Nazi-dominated mountains, somewhere in Germany for training on how to behave as prisoners of war.

We were trucked uphill over a dirt road. After several hours, we stopped next to a Nazi interrogation building. Their swastikas were on high stone-walled gateposts at the entrance. As we decamped, I noticed a strange silence. We were at the top of a mountain and there were no sounds except for the breeze on that late summer afternoon. The forest was coldly silent, emanating a sense of absolute lifelessness. It was desolate and eerie. We were marched along the dirt road for several miles. It got dark out and there were no lights. Then we were ordered to wait several hours before marching back to the interrogation building. During the march, I noticed a river flowing between the crevice between our mountain and another. The thin ribbon shined with a silver glow in the still moonlight. It must be the River Styx, I thought. There were gravestones near the dirt road that had swastikas next to the names. A dark pall existed over the entire still forest.

Finally, we were back in the interrogation building, tired, worn out, and ready to tell all. We marched past an office into a large central room which was entirely bare except for wooden benches against the right wall. The floors were dirt. The cells were to the left side and we were stripped down to our shorts and placed into the cells, a dozen to each. The dirt floor met a slate wall for urination to a drain at the bottom. There we spent the night before being singly interrogated in a room upstairs toward the rear. The next day, we were herded back to trucks and delivered to our unit in Baumholder.

The dirt floors absorbed blood and bodily fluids while victims were tortured on the benches. Remember Lawrence of Arabia when he was a Turkish prisoner? Same deal. The cells were temporary and minimal. According to our German resident barracks tailor, the forest had become silent because everybody had been starving in the aftermath of the war. They scoured the forest and hunted for anything that lived whether it flew, crawled, or ran from them. When they were finished, the forest was devoid of life. A place without life is desolate and unimaginably quiet. In this desolation rests the origin of their famine, the self-made Nazi torture chamber.

—⟶

Only man himself can create such horror and people succumb to the devils that create it. The Hell is man-made. We, as a nation, need to reflect on the choices we make during these times of plenty. Choices should be made to preserve and treasure our culture and world, not destroy it wantonly as we have been in pursuit of worshiping money, power and wealth at all costs.

Chapter Fourteen

Self-Resurrection

There are incredible, inexplicable powers and forces working through the ether reaching out and bringing miracles to selected individuals. Much clamor is made about people causing psychic events to occur, but sometimes they simply arrive because of a great human need.

Many years ago, Susan B. was a registered nurse working in the surgery department of a hospital. She was tall, highly intelligent, and was rapidly ascending the ranks of nursing credentials while also advancing her education towards higher goals. Each year when I saw her, I was reminded of Amelia Earhart because of her appearance and drive. She was highly skilled and was an excellent asset to surgical teams. Around that time, she had been suffering from body pains and scheduled minor surgery in her own hospital. The laparoscopy procedure was not considered to be life-threatening—the surgeon would merely be entering the abdominal cavity to complete the excision and hopefully, find the source of the pains.

Susan wasn't too concerned. The nurse, the anesthesiologist, and the doctor on the operating team were all experienced co-workers and she trusted them entirely. She saw no danger with the proposed routine surgery and lost no sleep over it. That was before the dream. Three days before the surgery, she went to sleep peacefully, her mind occupied only by thoughts of her children and husband. That night's sleep was restless, however, and she twisted in discomfort as a nightmare gripped her.

She found herself in the operating room. She recognized the doctor, the anesthesiologist, and nurse who were all staring down at her body on the operating room table. Susan was on the table, yet she was watching the scene from above as if it were an out-of-body experience. She began panicking as the realization struck her.

"She's dead," they were saying. There were tears in their eyes as they stood over her restrained thrashing body, helpless.

She woke and screamed at her husband, shaking him awake, "There's something wrong with the surgery. I saw it in a dream."

"Go back to sleep," he moaned, rubbing his eyes awake. "You know it's an easy one."

But the night remained a restless one. Her mind raced from one doubt to another, worrying about how much truth lay with the nightmare. Had it been merely a bad dream? Or could it have actually been a vision forewarning of the future? If it was a vision, how could she prevent it? She thought about canceling the surgery, but to do so for so silly a reason as a mere dream would have been illogical and embarrassing. She came up with a better idea.

The following day, Susan telephoned the surgical team to alert them regarding an unknown danger with the surgery. They dismissed her dream as nonsense, but she was unyielding and decided that she should fortify the team with another nurse and another doctor whom she knew.

Over the course of the next two days, she pulled all the strings she could tug on to get this doctor and nurse admitted into the operating room regardless if that was a violation of a normal protocol and costs. And to play safe, she ordered the crash cart to be placed at the operating room door in case of emergency.

When she was wheeled into the room on a gurney several days later, the room was full of medical friends and co-workers she knew and trusted. They all smiled warily and assured her that she would be okay—considering that the surgery was an easy one. There was one person who she didn't recognize. A surgical resident introduced herself, saying that she had been brought in to join the surgical team. She appreciated the gesture but hadn't expected this new doctor. A grim and nervous apprehension crept upon her as she was sedated, and her lights went out.

During the procedure, the new doctor injected carbon dioxide into her abdomen to separate her organs, making the surgical process easier. However, she miscalculated the needle's positioning and injected gas directly into a vein. A few moments later, the anesthetist noticed a heart murmur and the carbon dioxide level in the patient's blood had significantly elevated. It was likely that this held no meaning. However, it could also be a telltale sign of serious trouble. The anesthetist alerted the doctor of the possibility and, preemptively, called for the crash cart.

The cart arrived not a moment too soon. The injected gas reached Susan's brain and caused a spontaneous nervous system shutdown and she began thrashing on the table. The team responded quickly; immediately realizing the source of the problem.

"Use the restraints!" a doctor yelled as he reached for the crash cart.

Then, Susan's heart stopped.

As her life teetered on the pendulum between life and death, Susan saw a brilliant, white light illuminating her being. A wave of warmth and love overcame her, washing away all her worries and imbuing her with a peace that surpassed all comprehension. *This is what heaven feels like,* Susan realized. She found herself overwhelmed by the desire to stay and enjoy the serenity forever. She did not want to leave. Perhaps there was no reason to labor with such effort to stay on the Earth, after all.

The spirits, however, thought otherwise and a sudden jolt from the defibrillator ended her trek into the netherworld. From there, thanks to the anesthetist that she had chosen, the team proceeded to save Susan's life from what had only been meant to be a simple, safe procedure.

Being saved, however, didn't mean an immediate recovery. Susan spent the next week on a ventilator. After her recovery, she decided to continue her education with a new focus on life, realizing that she must have been saved for a specific purpose. She now wanted to teach nursing instead of practicing the profession. She saw life as more valuable and important during the coming years and went on to complete a Master's Degree and then a Doctorate. As the months passed, Susan became more religious, having been touched by her experiences in saving patients and by her own experience of having been saved.

One day, after graduating with the doctorate, she came to show me several offers for executive and teaching positions. One offer was from an accredited religious college that I had worked with, many years earlier, when they used my first book as a textbook (American Independent Business). They were starting a nursing program. "Take this school," I insisted. "You will love it. They have small classroom sizes and the Scriptures are over all the doors. The people are dedicated and wonderful to work with." She listened to me and never looked back afterward.

Susan has now worked there for years as an administrator and instructor. She was not particularly religious before, with the pressure of family, work, and education, but is now involved with Christian missionary work. She loves working there, even though she wouldn't call it "work" because it is her calling. Not too long ago, Susan directed the opening of a Master's program in nursing and then the new Doctor of Nursing Practice program at the university where she is now teaching many students medical techniques to save lives as professionals. She has been instrumental in changing a small Baptist College operating out of an old sanatorium building into a sprawling university. To this day, she holds the memory of the dream that saved her life close to her heart, inspiring her towards a meaningful future. And, yes, there are missionaries to foreign lands to spread the word of her newfound faith.

There are times when the spirits reach out from the ether to save us for the important things we can do for humanity. They have many ways through which they attempt to reach out to us. Perhaps, we should pay more attention to our dreams, especially when, instead of rehashing the day's events, the guardian spirits are posting a warning for the future, the results of which would be life-changing and humanitarian. Her silver thread did not break, and she has accomplished wonders in return.

Chapter Fifteen

You've been Dead Before

B ill D., a Cherokee aircraft flight test engineer, was riding his ten-speed bike one morning near his house in Southern California. He was 37-years old, highly intelligent, and in great shape, which is why he was riding at top speed around the mountain after work. Suddenly, a car came up from behind Bill, hitting and tossing him head over heels over the car. As he flew through the air, he was conscious enough to look back to see if another car was coming to run him over again. He landed on the pavement, on outstretched hands and knees rolling over, propelled backward by the momentum. While still pushed by the energy of the fall, he managed to hold his arm out to feel the dirt roadside shoulder and roll into it, getting off the road. Then, he blacked out.

He woke up in a state of sensory deprivation. Everything was fuzzy, and he was unable to feel any of his surrounds. It felt as though he was stranded, floating above a void. The atmosphere was hazy and pleasant but lacking in brightness and it was as big as the Universe. Bill saw people floating by in a state of serenity. Some people held clipboards like in his office. Some couples floated by happily. It was soundless, tasteless, weightless, painless, lifeless, and devoid of touch; only with his sight and mind.

He turned from the wondrous scene and saw a golden thread trailing from his left fingertips to his right fingertips. On one side of the thread was his awareness of himself and the way he saw people. He felt that it was his Freudian id-ego, or love of himself, being presented at this time. On the other side of the golden thread was his family and friends who were in his life, but he felt they didn't know how much he loved them. He became aware that he needed to reach out to them and tell them how much he really loved them. An instant later, a serene awareness came over him as he saw a pedestal by an arch with a voice, a wondrous friendly voice, of his best friend, Jesus or God talking to him. The voice of awareness was not so much a voice as it was a thought—rather than hearing it through his ears, he felt its message spread through his mind and body. It asked, "Are you ready to go now?" He instantly thought of his family and friends below the gold thread and knew he didn't want to leave them. He answered the voice and felt a warm, understanding approval spread through his being. Then, the scene shifted.

Bill found himself hovering over the scene of the accident. He looked down and saw the paramedics working on his body. They had gotten there ten minutes after the accident and had found him dead, without any respiration or pulse. They immediately tried to resuscitate him with one paramedic working on his chest to help him breathe while the other used a breathing pump. After about ten minutes, the chest paramedic sat up saying, "He's dead. Let's call it." The other responder nodded. He quit giving Bill CPR and straightened up as well, fatigued with the efforts to save him. Bill, looking down from outside his body, observed both responders emotionally charged facial expressions suddenly change to frozen wooden, puppet-like automatons. Something had suddenly taken over their bodies. Completely void of expression they both renewed the resuscitation process with one working Bill's chest again while the other automatically held the pump mask to his face. Bill watched them tirelessly working without a sound or signal between them. After a period of time which could not be measured, Bill felt air fill his lungs, his pulse returned, and the responders' faces came back to life with emotion and excitement. He was bandaged and rushed off to the hospital. He had no broken bones but had serious bleeding and contusions from skidding along the pavement on his back, head, and legs. His great physical condition had helped save him. Bill ended up spending the next four months recuperating.

In the hospital, the responders would tell Bill that they didn't remember going back to work on him the second time. God had been there to save Bill. It was a miracle that saved him. For a full 20 minutes, he had been dead and yet, somehow, his silver thread had not broken.

Bill's legs were so bruised, swollen, and torn that the paramedics had to bandage his legs to keep him from bleeding to death. He was in a wheelchair for months afterward without the use of his legs and was told that he would never walk again. He was determined that he would never spend his life in a wheelchair and after months of intensive therapy the determined and strong-minded man succeeded against the odds.

Afterward, Bill decided to study his death and revival. He found it hard to reconcile the near-death experiences that he read about with his actual death experience. He read up on paranormal experiences and became an expert on himself and the experience. However, he always remained in wonder at the miracle that he had been saved by Jesus or God. He had extensive experience as a Vietnam veteran working with PTSD traumatized combat veterans and helped them bring many back from the edges of psychosis. This had conditioned him to other people's problems but never his own. He was very much more outgoing with people afterward and not afraid to let people know how he felt about them. He realized that words of kindness—such as "love"—were not to be miserly guarded but rather, were to be shared magnanimously.

One day, he was at a conference retreat, in a room full of strangers, when he noticed a middle-aged person across the room standing aside from the crowd. There seemed to be a lime-green aura emanating from the man and, as Bill observed the man, he became more and more certain that this man was like him. When the opportunity presented itself, Bill approached him.

"You've been dead," Bill announced with an outreached hand to the stranger.

"You too," the man returned with a great smile.

They talked for a while, exchanging experiences common with people who have died and returned. It appeared to each other that they both had the same auras, lime-green with a tint of orange on the outside fuzzy edge. The other man, a County Sheriff, had been diagnosed with incurable advanced-stage cancer a while back. One night, however, he woke to find a stranger sitting on the hospital bed beside him. "Your cancer will be gone in the morning," the stranger said and disappeared. The next morning, the County Sheriff woke to find that the cancer was gone. But his cancer's disappearance wasn't the only thing that intrigued everyone in the room—the Sheriff had also died in the middle of the night, right around the time he believed he had seen the stranger. The man that Bill greeted was actually the conference speaker who had come to talk about returning to life after death.

Bill's right arm always ached for reasons unknown. Over the years, he had told many doctors about his arm, but no one had been able to cure it, so he learned to live with it. One day, he was in an airplane hangar with other engineers when he met a man that he recognized as a Native American Indian. Bill, who is a tall Cherokee, spoke to him and found him to be a Navajo medicine man. The Navajo had recognized Bill as an Indian because of his high cheekbones and facial features. The Navajo told Bill that he knew him to have died before and that he needed some stones to set on his path. The medicine man produced a small pouch of smooth rocks and placed them in Bill's hands.

Then, he told Bill, "I also know that your arm is hurting. Let me help you. Hold your arms down and loose." Bill did so. Then, the Navajo held his arms straight out and motioned from head to toe over Bill's body from behind. His hands were about an inch away from Bill as he moved them from head to foot. With a yell and a clap of hands, the Navajo stepped back smiling. "Well? How do you feel now?"

Bill moved his arm and tested it by stretching for a minute. Soon after that, he realized that the pain had disappeared. He looked at his fellow Brave, "I don't feel anything at all. That was wonderful!" Afterward, they parted company. To this day, Bill still has the little bag of rocks and memories of the healing stranger who made his pain go away forever.

On the highways of life, there are many strangers who have had a chance to cross over but chose not to. They're still here to greet you, shake your hand, and wish you another good life. Those of us who are fortunate enough to be saved are all better off after our body recovers our silver thread. Not many are invited to the dark side of death, but I know of a few. Fortunately, those are only a few individuals in the thousands of people I know. Life in any form is precious and we share it with all the other living breathing beings in the universe. Make the most of your fragile silver strand of thread.

Chapter Sixteen

Karma

Our present-day lives are so interwoven with threads of memories from the past and thoughts of the future that correlations between events can be hard to recognize or verify; until they prove true. There is a great deal of logic involved in correctly reasoning with the information provided by the etheric spirits or those spiritual people who are especially in tune with those spirits. Sometimes, information is given which can be verified by other parties, like the Watergate reporting. "Verify by a second party," Mr. Woodward, the Watergate reporter for the Washington Post, was told. *Verify*. But how does one verify or prove Karmic events? Can one really believe in Karma—an abstraction of past, present, and future? How does one access Karma?

I have known many psychic individuals. I have known good ones and bad ones. Recently, a relative went to one in Temecula, and the first thing the psychic did was to ask for his occupation. Had she been truly psychic, she would have known his occupation without asking. It is best to use references for a good psychic because there are many phonies out there. This chapter is about Karma through psychics.

⁓

Clairvoyants are most well known for their ability to peruse the future for information through a medium spiritual presence. Many, however, are also quite capable of reading the present and are asked to find misplaced objects, search for long-lost relatives, or investigate the minds of alleged criminals for hints toward incriminating evidence. Even more intriguing, others claim to be capable of reading the past of an individual's soul—pasts that extend beyond a single lifespan. This is where the assumption and correction of sins from past lives come into play in what is often referred to as 'Karma'. Karma is also the basis of most of the Asian religions and Buddhism which focuses on changing from self-interest to spiritual values. In other words, it focuses on changing one's selfishness to universality.

I have three experiences, relating to Karma that is worth mentioning:

The first was one that involves my first wife Betty. She was from Scotland and was very thin when I first met her at age 20. We fell in love and she later moved to England with her family. Since I was in the Army, she had to go to an American airbase in England for a physical and to complete medical exams. They told her she had a hole in her heart and that she could not be considered for a visa to America.

She, somehow, was admitted to the Oxford Medical University Hospital. They offered her treatment by open heart surgery but, because this was only 1959, it came with a mere 50/50 success rate. She was the first patient in England to have this surgery at the time. Because she was in love, she opted for the experimental surgery, hoping that fortune would be with her.

The operation was a complete success and, afterward, she was able to put on weight, was allowed to marry me, immigrated to America, and gained citizenship.

I met my Scottish wife as a result of a chain of events which began when I boarded a flight from North Carolina to Frankfort, Germany for my next duty station. The flight was aborted to Prestwick, Scotland when weather conditions over Germany turned sour. I met my future wife that night in a nearby Troon coffee shop. She worked for the Robert Louis Stevenson bookstore which was managed by his elegant and refined granddaughter who would have employees read all the new books so they could tell customers about the books' contents. What I didn't know at the time was that this was the Ayer Provence where my ancestor, Robert 'The Bruce', was born many years before.

A year later, I was visiting her in Scotland while on leave from Germany when we decided to marry. Her family moved to Reading England where she went to an US Airbase for a physical, but they wouldn't give her permission to marry me or visit the US until her heart valve anomaly was corrected. Six months after her surgery at Oxford University, we went to the US Embassy in Trafalgar Square in London with marriage documents in hand. Outside on the cobblestone streets, Queen Elizabeth II and French General Charles de Gaulle tore past on a gilded open carriage drawn by magnificent white horses straight out of a Cinderella movie. They were sitting erect and staring forward to the front seat, Charles in a brown uniform with his tall stovepipe hat made him about seven or eight feet tall, and Elizabeth beside him bedazzling in jewels and attire befitting a Queen. Both were stoic lifeless figures of power and state.

After we were married by a Justice of the Peace, on another leave, we visited my family estate, The Vyne, near London and nearby the magnificent estate of the Duke of Wellington, the victor of the Battle of Waterloo, with the help of a German Army under Prussian Prince Von Blucher. Inside the huge foyer of the estate manor, a hundred or more absolutely magnificent French Napoleonic battle flags hung in silent splendor, row, upon row, from end to end of the great hall. Even greater was a surprise in the huge stone barn that housed the Duke's 'Death Wagon'. It was a gigantic wagon with its sides cast from the bronze of captured French cannons. Battle scenes were beautifully depicted on every surface. When the Duke died, the Death Wagon was hauled around London by a royal platoon of horses with his coffin inside.

Years later, a client of mine recommended a psychic to me and out of curiosity I decided to pay the seer a visit. The psychic brought up a past life situation which involved me as a figure of authority and my future wife as a servant who had stolen something. Although it had been a minor crime, the punishment at the time was death. My past self had been very reluctant to follow the law but, ultimately, had no choice. This had been in ancient times and the punishment would have been a sword through the heart—the most merciful way to go. The psychic advised that she had come back to me and I was to support and take care of her in this life. Afterward, I believed that the hole in her heart could have been inherited in Karmic fashion and through me, the doctors would be able to repair it and she would have a normal life. And we did live together, peacefully, for many years afterward.

I have always had an open mind for spiritual matters, even though I can be very different about business. With an open mind comes broad understanding, which is why I visited selected psychics.

Another psychic told me that she glimpsed another one of my past lives where I was an old man, living alone in the forest. The elderly man was always coughing and would often go outside of his cold cabin for firewood. Eventually, the area around his cabin was picked clean and he began returning to his fire with only twigs and small branches. He did not live much longer.

Years later, another psychic looked into my past and saw the same old man—a pathetic person, coughing and searching for scarce firewood. He found nothing worthwhile and his futile struggle came to a cold, lonely conclusion.

This psychic, too, had seen a man of bad karma. How two different people could see the same image is beyond my imagination. It was clear, however, that they did see the same image and that could easily have been a representation of my real karma. After all, I was born asthmatic and have been coughing all my life, off and on.

I have found in my many years, that there is a huge learning curve on the journey from childhood to adulthood and then beyond to, what I call, the age of wisdom. Our individual karma is also lived by way of a learning curve; outside of inherited blessings and problems we are born with, we make many mistakes as we mature both physically and mentally. Along the way, we can only hope to correct our mistakes and find the straight road through life, afterward.

The greatest truth is that of Moses' Ten Commandments, the wisdom of which covers most of the events in life that we must learn before we leave. I find the Bible to be a great history book which covers not only worldwide ancient events but also definitions of good and evil for mankind. After we reach the Age of Wisdom, we will have a vast understanding and awareness of people and humanity in general. It will be a great age for all. You and I will be able to look around corners and see all the repetitions of reality. Hopefully, by then, we will see kindness met with understanding and be able to perceive and understand madness should it ever be present.

The Karma of my wife's earlier death was repaid when I saved her life years later at a Riverside restaurant. She began choking on her lunch and was unable to breathe. She fell to her knees and I hit her back dislodging the food that was trapped in her windpipe. She never returned to the restaurant chain after her brush with death.

In our travels through life, we encounter people who influence us in different ways. Maybe some of them are related to our Karmic past lives which we experience as *déjà vu*— an inexplicable familiarity—, and others simply by chance.

One day at my Riverside, California office, a client introduced his friend and fellow insurance agent, who was visiting from Las Vegas. His friend was middle-aged, had an established business, and had a story to tell. In the movie *Gone With The Wind*, Rhett Butler was parading downtown with his baby, Bonnie, and was showing her around in her beautiful, large wheeled baby carriage and giving adios and broad smiles to the ladies on the porches during this hot Georgia day. It was a beautiful show with happy people abounding, Rhett at his handsome best, and the beautiful baby girl Bonnie.

That day, the producers of the film were undecided about which child to portray as the baby girl Bonnie. They decided, instead, on a photogenic baby boy. The real Bonnie in the carriage was the insurance agent standing in front of me. Yes, Bonnie was a boy, at least in this scene before she/he grew up.

Another interesting meeting was at a restaurant in Upland, California. I had published my first book, American Independent Business, and had been elected to be the editor of the morning breakfast Kiwanis Club. Under the pen name "The Scribe", I won many awards for the club with its little bulletin. When I first joined the club, the bulletin was a dull, lifeless four-page placemat left behind by the large membership after breakfast. I stepped over the line with the bulletin, making it accurate and bringing the membership into it with a humor appreciated only in a men's club. The members would now bring their copy home for their families to enjoy. Once a week, in the early morning before work, we would meet at a restaurant and other restaurant patrons would listen in to the meetings to join in the laughter and good-natured events between members.

One morning, I was approached by a very tall and gaunt man who seemed vaguely familiar. He introduced himself as Howard Hughes' double. I was surprised, never realizing that rich famous people, especially celebrities, have people who show up at the front door for the photojournalists and paparazzi, while the target goes elsewhere. This soft-spoken, casually dressed, elderly man was a professional diversion. As a matter of introduction, he stated that Howard was a brilliant but eccentric man who had medical problems and adored privacy. The stand-in loved working for Howard but was not really interested in telling me about his career.

He had a written a screenplay and wanted me to read it. We agreed to meet at the next Kiwanis meeting where he would lend it to me. We parted company as instant friends. The next week, he handed me his screenplay, neatly typed and bound. I promised to bring it back a week later with my comments. He was all smiles because a screenplay or book is a gestation of great amounts of labor and mental application.

I read the play during the next week and am sorry to say that I don't even remember the name of it. The work was about 150-pages long, double-spaced, and in an easy to read in script format. The story took place in a bar and mostly revolved around a beautiful man in rich nightclubs, beautiful girls, and a lavishly adorned apartment. The plot was missing. It brought to mind the post-WWII days of movies when actors were under contract to produce weekly or monthly movies and they all seemed too similar. They were almost serialized with the same actors, same places, same themes, and the same cocktails in double-breasted suits facing nightgown dressed women. Plots were secondary to the parade of familiar, adorned actors in cigarette smoke filled settings. The screenplay was a story from a man who had been surrounded by the epic industry which had focused on a glamorous era of fantasy which poor Depression-weary families subscribed to before and after the long war. The period of the avant-garde films had passed, leaving a lonely man shopping his story forever. I returned the script and confessed that the story was pleasant but rather dated. He left and I never saw him again.

Sometimes, Karma or casualty brings the nicest people in and out of our lives, leaving us to live on with only the memories of them, like two trains passing in the night. There is a powerful rush of energy and then an empty vacuum.

All these things combine to fulfill the karma of the past and prepare the karma of the future. Count your blessings and stand above all the silliness and scams that are pervasive throughout today's society. Be on guard, be yourself, and know when to trust that you are right.

This is my perspective on karma—a perspective that came through the etheric spirits. The spirits willingly give us special powers of knowledge, so long as we open our mind to accept them. I believe that we are born with God-given, natural talents or endowed with them from genetic or karmic sources, but the gifts don't end there—they also influence our powers later in life. It is up to us, individually, to develop these powers because we are all different and unique. If you love to play the violin, then try to be a great violinist. If you are a math whiz, you might reach your maximum potential by becoming an accountant or mathematician. If you have a great voice, then develop this power which is unique to you. Bring out the greatness you are blessed with. When people say, "God bless you", I believe they usually mean it. In this respect, we live forever with the help of the etheric spirits. Didn't Jesus once say that Heaven is on Earth? To go a step further, Joseph Campbell studied world religions and published famous works showing that there are common elements between people and religions all over the world. It appears that there is a common spirit or influence for mankind. This is the etheric spirit.

Chapter Seventeen

Angels on the Highway of Life

E very time an aircraft crashes, the headlines list the number of dead and we mourn for them while considering ourselves lucky to have not been on that flight. Yet, we all drive an average of a thousand miles each month and are subject to much more casualty per mile in a car than on any flight. Our etheric journey exposes us to much danger on the road.

A new client brought me tax return data for her neighbors. It was a stressful meeting—the whole family had been in an auto accident which was not their fault. The neighbor's car had been hit by a reckless speeder and completely totaled, killing everybody. There were newspaper headlines showing the car engulfed in flames. I have done many tax returns for deceased family members of clients but never before for a good neighbor looking after her late friends. We actually don't have control whatsoever of death pending and can only hope we have kept our peace with God and the spirits. Better yet, it is wonderful to have really kind neighbors who will support you in life and death. We no longer have tribes to look after our well-being, but we need to keep the neighbors close.

who will support you in life and death. We no longer have tribes to look
after our well-being, but we need to keep the neighbors close.

After I left the military, my family went on vacation to New Hampshire where my sister lived. We headed north from Boston in my little 1962 Buick Special station wagon. A few days later we were in the beautiful White Mountain terrain which skiers love and lumber companies exploit. We drove among the pines, hills, and mountains until we ended at Mount Washington, the highest mountain in the state. We decided to drive up the mountain instead of taking an ancient cog railway and started out on a graded narrow road which wound around the mountainsides. After an hour, we were at the top, completely shrouded in fog-like clouds and no visibility. No view at all except for the stone weather station building on top. No McDonald's or Bay State Gas Stations. No people either, even at the windy, cold, and desolate station.

We turned around and headed downhill to civilization. The car had old-fashioned drum brakes, which were typical before sports car disc brakes became standard equipment on most cars. We headed down the winding narrow mountain road and the brakes suddenly didn't act right. They were heating up and working too hard. It became harder and harder to slow the car enough for safe driving. I knew I would never make it to the bottom alive. I looked in the back seat from my mirror and my father, the tough silent forever type, had fear written into his eyes. That was the only time I ever saw him afraid of anything. I spotted a space ahead of us on the inside of the road with a big boulder at the end and aimed for it. I literally stood on the brake pedal to stop the wagon, not knowing if I would crash into the boulder or not. We were lucky because the car screeched to a stop just short of the rock. We all got out, walked around, worry vanished into silent joy as we waited, with the hood up, for the brakes to cool for the other half of the trip. Paratroopers take lots of chances but this time I needed help from my guardian spirits to survive the dangerous drive with my family.

❧

Many years ago, I bought the first Subaru Sedan. It was really a red beer can designed to look like a car. A week after the 10,000-mile warranty ran out, the head gasket leaked and caused a major engine job. I hated the car which sported broken locks, tube-type tires after the whole world had switched to tubeless, and overall, was a sheet metal nightmare. But it was cheap, and I was poor. One night, I was returning from college when a car bumped my rear quarter-panel. I veered away from the old Pontiac, which weighed twice as much as my tin can, but he bumped me again. I got ahead of him and pulled over to the side of the road to get out of his drunken way.

Then, bang! He hit the back of the Subaru at fifty MPH. My car spun around and tossed me out the door. The drunken driver pulled over only because his fender on my side was crushed. The Subaru was totaled, and I was dizzied from the shock. My glasses had disappeared. I stood next to the car to get my senses back until a CHP car arrived. The officers checked the site, took pictures, and breathalyzed the drunken driver of the Pontiac. I found out later from the reports that his alcohol level was .16. Somehow, I got home and back to work the next morning as if nothing had happened. I was unscathed and glad to be alive. That evening I got a call at home from the reckless driver who was in the hospital with internal injuries. He was trying to blame me for the accident. Sometimes the etheric angels are by our side, but the fools still remain among us. My insurance company called and found a replacement Subaru for me. After some negotiation, I rejected their offer and bought a better car.

<hr />

When driving home from work on the freeway one summer evening a swarm of bees enveloped my car in a dark cloud of buzzing wings. They came out of nowhere from the left side of the road crossing the freeway to begin a new hive, which is what bees do when they get a new queen and the old home gets crowded. It was really scary and terrifying to be surrounded by thousands of bees. Fortunately, because it was hot outside, my windows were closed with the A/C on. If my window had been open, I would have had a car full of bees while driving at 70 MPH. I doubt if I would have been able to maintain control and probably would have spun out of control. When I got home I hosed the car down to get the hundreds of dead bees out of the radiator, wiper blades, and grill works. Again, I thank my spirits that the encounter wasn't more serious.

Years later, I was driving down the freeway from San Bernardino when I noticed a huge black SUV next to me in the right lane. He got ahead of me and I decided to pass him and get away from the bus-sized vehicle. Suddenly, he turned into my lane as I was passing him. My car, a little BMW convertible, was probably hard to see because it was much smaller than the BUF "Big Ugly Fella the pilots used to say of the B-52 SAC nuclear bombers from the airbase nearby". According to my wife, I exclaimed something like, "Jesus!" as I made a hard, left turn. A moment later, I was looking at the fence separating the paths of the freeway and I turned it hard right to correct. In two seconds, I had turned into the next lane at 70 MPH flawlessly, without rolling over, and I was now looking at the car in front of me. The BUF was now next to me. He would have caused a huge collision if I hadn't moved quickly. The etheric Spirits, my guardian, or Jesus were all showing me how to drive that day. And I had the perfect car to do it with and still have that car in my garage where it will stay as long as I live.

Recently, I rented a Chrysler van for a vacation with my wife, Nett, and grandson. When we put the contract in the glove box, we noticed that there was no owner's manual. Several days later, we were at Zion National Park in a line forming outside the huge unlighted tunnel through the mountain. The line started up and suddenly was moving at forty-five MPH into the 10-mile tunnel. Everybody was switching their headlights on, and because the gear shift lever was on the steering post, I tried turning the lever on the left side and got only directional lights. It was panic time as the people in front of me pulled away while I was still fishing for headlight switches. The dashboard didn't have any additional controls for lights, high beams, anything. I had to keep up with the traffic in front of me, afraid to go fast or slow down because the car behind me would hit me. We were in panic and terror with no lights except the faint directional light flashing off the right side of the stone wall on the right. The front traffic kept pulling away and their tail lights were off in the distance. For more than five minutes, because the tunnel was miles long, we drove in extremely stressed circumstances expecting to hit the wall at any moment with absolutely no control over our situation. Miraculously, we got to the other side of the forever tunnel, pulled over to study the dash and finally found a toggle switch, low on the dash next to the steering column. It turned the headlights on. All the saints in heaven must have been with us that day and the etheric forces bringing their benevolence to our presence. I still wonder how we survived that trip. Some would call it luck or faith, but I have always felt I have had a spirit on my shoulders helping me live another day with my family.

I always seem to be in harm's way. Maybe I should count my blessings and say a prayer to God, to the etheric spirits, and to my guardian before I go anywhere. But in between, I work hard to be worthy of their benevolence.

Chapter Eighteen

Speaking to God

A highly successful client had a problem. Fred C., like most entrepreneurs, spent day and night with his business—in this case, a prosperous regional Rock & Roll music radio station. During the first years of their marriage, his young wife, Jane C., helped in the office and was quite happy. They built a huge studio-office building and moved into a house next door. As the years wore on, however, the business' increasing and incessant demands for time and effort stole quality family life with their two children. Despite an upgraded home, a mansion on a hill in town, Jane grew irritable and reluctant to work. She didn't like the huge house they lived in—after all, what is the point of a mansion if the whole family were never around to enjoy it?

She quit the business and returned to nursing school which she had abandoned when she married. The radio station's advertising revenue declined with the recession of 1989 and as prospects of the once-prosperous business drifted away, she drifted even further away from her husband. She fell in love with an instructor and moved in with him, leaving her children with her husband and his father, who was living with him in the mansion. Then, her lover was murdered.

Jane moved in with relatives, blaming her husband for the gruesome shooting, and reluctantly visited her children at the mansion.

⌒

This is an excerpt from my book, Rock & Roll Murders:

⌒

That evening, Jane wanted to die. She sat in a stuffed chair at her aunt's alone, crying. The lights went out when her aunt went to bed. A night-light glowed on a wall. Jane fell asleep. She dreamed that she visited God. He had blondish-brown hair and a beard. His trimmed white robes flowed and blew about His ethereal presence. There was a wondrous white light about and behind Him which filled the air. He stood in mid-air, barefoot, holding out long arms to her-- His long fingers reached for her. Jane felt at peace and floated in the presence of God. There was no facial movement as He spoke without speaking. He was supreme, overpowering, but had a calm voice. "I'm here for you. Come to me if you are ready." *Jane immediately realized that she was dying and would leave the boys without a mother. She chose to live and suddenly the dream was gone, and she woke up. She now felt alive and energized, ready to go on with her life, ready to do what she had to do for survival.*

This was exactly how Jane described her meeting with God. He rescued her from her death wish with a solution for life. Hopefully, if you ever reach into the depths of despair, the etheric spirits will find you as God did for this lady and help you correct your course in life. They are the good forces in the face of the evil the world has to offer. In Asian culture, this is represented by the Yin and Yang, opposing spirits of good and evil facing each other in a circle of life. I have never reached out for the Spirits in prayer, but they find me when I need them. They are always there for you if you look hard enough or need them in an instant of life or death. Life-threatening events always surround us and after it is over, we say, "Gosh, did that really happen?" Accordingly, we need to look back and thank our blessings and those spirits who save us when needed. Be aware that we are never alone.

Jane moved back in with her husband—the only source of income and home for the family—and began to believe her husband's story of innocence. Years passed, and the business was sold. But, ultimately, her husband was tried and convicted of murder. Millions of dollars in legal fees ate at the wealth that was once there and Jane moved out of town with an employee. She always carried a loaded shotgun in the trunk of her car.

Other clients have had encounters with God. Hal had died on the operating room table and drifted into the spiritual tunnel of weightlessness and painless journey into the beautiful heaven ahead. In the tunnel, he met God who was ahead of him. God spoke, "Are you ready now?" Hal thought of his wife who was ill and needed his support; his son who he would dearly miss, and that his taxes needed to be done. He responded that, although his life was painful, he would like to go back and take care of his affairs first. He immediately woke up on the operating room table with the anesthetic wearing off. The next month, he came in for his taxes and told me about his trip to heaven. Within a year, his wife passed on. Not long afterward, he went to join her. He was a wonderful person, always dedicated to maintaining his home and family. It appears he was able to defer his death and extend his tenure on Earth another year for unfinished business. He was able to control his future like so many others, because he was a good person who simply asked for more time here. That was 25-years ago, and his son still visits once a year.

Chapter Nineteen

Village Healer

After a very serious melanoma operation and being given less than a 50/50 chance of survival, I visited the Philippines with my wife. No matter where I went, the people were always friendly and accommodating. The climate with humid heat and dense smog was almost unbearable. The closeness of all the family members was an unmistakable attribute of their survival economy. One day, my wife announced that she and a friend would be going to a healer in the provinces—villages that lay out in the countryside, far from the cities and their terrible, smoggy atmosphere.

Transportation in that country is very different from what it is like here. Everything in the city and outlying suburbs is crowded. All the men wear T-shirts because they are inexpensive and ideal in such a hot, humid place. Travel is by *jeepney*, a type of miniature bus privately owned and operated by the driver and is usually colorfully adorned, no two alike. Most burn a cheap, dirty, sulfurous type of diesel which adds greatly to the pollution that chokes people everywhere.

So, we started off in a jeepney to a bus stop where we took a big bus to the provinces. It was a great trip through the countryside filled with palms and square rice farms where many people worked alongside oxen locally called *carabaos*, pulling logs with chains instead of tractors. Ancient, terraced rice paddies covered mountainsides in the distance. They were a sight to behold from thousands of years of constant cultivation; they were still worked in the primitive fashion. There were few factories or industry of any kind. Agriculture appeared to be everything in this economy.

We left the highway and the land changed to jungle and native huts, all with sheet metal roofs and old tires lying on top to hold the roofs down when the winds pick up. Sometimes, there were no nails to hold the roofs down and only the weight of the tires kept them in place. After a long ride and then another tricycle ride through dirt roads lined with coconut palms, banana trees, bird of paradise plants big as trees, we arrived at the center of a little village. Across the street was a small hut with a large porch crowded with villagers sitting on benches patiently waiting for their turn to see the healer inside. We walked past the tricycles parked around the entrance and found a seat among the staring patients.

After a few minutes, a thin elderly man, who reminded me of Mahatma Gandhi, exited the room in the back. He led a small girl and her mother out, then surveyed the crowd. He spotted us foreigners and motioned us in like special guests or patients. I felt guilty that we were being admitted ahead of the local people who may have been waiting hours in the humid heat but because he knew Nanette's friend, he insisted that we headed inside.

The room had a simple wooden table and a matching set of chairs. A large, colored poster of a movie star covered much of the wall for all to appreciate like a political poster, attesting to his ability of to reach out to the famous in need of his special healing powers. The lady who brought us here was the first to engage his services. He stretched his hands and placed them on her shoulders, passed over her stomach and then her head. He spoke to her in Tagalog, which of course I did not understand a word. Nor did I understand anything when he did the same for my wife.

Then, it was my turn and Nanette translated briefly: "I had been sick, had been very wealthy, and was still very ill."

After speaking those words, the elderly man produced a stainless-steel kidney dish with surgical instruments lying in it, indicating "surgery". He spent a lot of time with his hands on my head and pronounced that I would survive all. He produced small bottles of "sacred" palm oil healing solution for the ladies, which they bought in addition to the fee for the visit.

As we left, I could not help but notice that this man was the only person available for anybody's illness and yet they all had hope and smiled, seeing foreigners going so far just to visit him. He was their only hope. I believe he had the good psychic ability to absorb the past of his patients, but the future would speak for itself. A week later, I had a successful prostate surgery in a city hospital. Etheric spirits worked with me and, maybe, they worked with the little man in the village too. That was fifteen years ago.

Part of the healing process involves having the patient connect with the doctor for faith and hope as a source of successful outcomes. In this case, the man had a captive audience and was certainly successful in making people feel good and, in that way, they could be on the path to healing, as most illnesses pass away on their own. I am certain he also had local remedies handed-down over the ages. I would not vouch for future healing and certainly not hands-on healing. But the little man gave hope to the native villagers and the spirits were left to do the rest.

Before we left the island, we visited a Catholic charity medical facility also located in the provinces. The countryside was composed of narrow streets and dirt roads, but this large village had a much larger population than that of the healer's tiny village. The facility was fortified on all sides by ten-foot stone walls and, at the entrance, a guard stood watch. It was similar to a Spanish mission except the villagers worked in the mission which also functioned as a hospital- church.

Every morning, men would enter with a yoke of water pails on their shoulders to water the vegetable garden which occupied half of the court-yard. Part of the remainder was an outside chapel with religious icons and benches for people to practice their faith and to bless the patients inside. The patients were supported by the Catholic poor boxes from various churches. Patients were plucked right off the streets or brought by the patient's relatives when they had no available care or money for doctors. Basic medical attention was provided for the patients who had the freedom to ambulate or receive attention in the big ward. Rooms in small cottages were provided for private patients in the back.

These were experiences of a lifetime. I had seen a village psychic-healer taking care of the small villages where there were no medical services and, on the other side of the coin, I witnessed a Church providing services for the ill that came to them. No medical insurance, no doctors. The Philippines is famous for educating medical professionals. But they are exported, and remittances are returned to their families. This is an example of how Third World countries take care of their own. Only their faith and religion could provide comfort in these scenarios. God will always bless them, and they will survive in ways we cannot imagine.

Chapter Twenty

Suicide Bomber

The little Italian man had been my client for 35 years. Together, we had gone through IRS field audits, payroll tax audits, and sales tax audits. All the while, Vic P. had stayed married to the same wife and kept the pizza restaurant business alive. It started as a small business where you would pick up his Red Devil pizza from outside through a window. The Italians from Chicago had a monopoly on these little take-out restaurants and they were passed down through the generations, the same as Korean cleaners in Southern California. His business began with a single, humble room housing the oven which would burn you if you got too close. This was replaced by a more efficient oven, which cut back on gas fuel costs. Then it grew into a larger restaurant and then an even larger sit-down restaurant with beer and wine on the menu. Vic was smart, took chances, had girlfriends, conducted business at a nearby bar, hid things from the taxman, bought a big house on a hill, and lived the life of a successful entrepreneur.

One would never have guessed that once upon a time, he had been a member of the 82nd Airborne, during the Vietnam War. Same outfit as me but different war. My war was the peacetime war—the Cold War. Vic never said a word about it except that he abhorred the chicken-shit, the endless inspections, and the callous-disdain attitude the NCOs and officers had for their subordinates. The military had gone a long ways back from the earlier time when the men elected their NCOs. He served his three years faithfully but did not re-enlist.

He withdrew from the business to build custom luxury houses out of state. That venture was a disaster and the business declined in his absence. The business which he had grown from a sapling into a huge tree, was failing and he was tired of its demands. He sold the business and retired to visit his son, who is now a medical doctor living out of state, and relatives everywhere. One day, I kept after him and asked, "Everybody else has war stories, why not you?" He seemed hesitant to broach the topic but, after a little insistence, he explained that his job was top secret and he was not supposed to let anybody know what he did.

Nothing a couple beers couldn't solve, of course. One day after some beers, he told his story. He was stationed at Bragg with the 82nd for the whole three years of his enlistment during the Vietnamese War. Everybody else was sent there but he was held back. Maybe his high intelligence tests (GT scores) were an influence. If so, they liked blowing up their best people. Before the war, the Army demonstrated the Davy Crockett Mk-54 rocket—a small rocket fired from a recoilless rifle which could be set on a tripod on the ground or the back of a pickup truck, as in Somalia. The plutonium warhead weighed only 55 pounds, but the yield was low, not in kilotons but only 20 tons of TNT. Still more powerful than any blockbuster aerial bomb. Vic was attached to a unit which would jump with the airborne trooper version of the same device. It weighed 100 pounds in the insulated leather case he jumped with. He went out the door with it between his legs, like riding a steer in a rodeo. After hitting the ground and recovering his chute, he would strip it down to a bomb weighing 55 pounds. He would then wear a backpack with the bomb in it to go to the designated target. "Remember, we are in enemy territory, paratroopers are always surrounded," Vic reminded me. Then, he would place the charge, turn the timer-igniters up to 45 minutes and skedaddle. He made many jumps with the thing and dummy warheads but, ultimately, was never called into action. My research points to a Russian invasion of Germany which was the original plan. The Allies would throw everything they had into the Fulda Gap which would be crowded with invading thousands of Russian tanks heading to NATO Headquarters at Frankfurt, Germany.

It certainly was a suicide mission. I joked with Vic over it and told him he was the only suicide bomber I have ever known. He doesn't think it is funny and absolutely hated bailing out of a C-130 with that thing between his legs like Slim Pickens riding the hydrogen bomb down in Doctor Strangelove.

Vic's Statement: *"We had a reserve and weapon. Carried it between my legs and waddled like a duck with it between legs. Yes, it had two detonators. I had top secret clearance. Had to in the Green Berets units. I think the bomb weighed about 90 lbs., if I recall correctly. We would jump with it in a padded box. Land with it, take it out of the box. Then put it into our backpack, pack it to a given location of the enemy. It was to be used for big purposes, Big ops... Detonate it, then try to get out. If not, kiss your ass away..."*

Because he was never called on the mission, he survived the Vietnam War and the proposed European War with Russia. He has had his etheric angels and guardians in place for a long time. Firsthand, it kept him out of the Vietnam War which was raging all the time he was at Bragg and his outfit was always on frontline combat duty. It appears that the two

Airborne Divisions suffered nearly 50% casualties. Secondly, he was slated for a different war altogether, and never had to go there. He certainly survived by default. Call it luck or his etheric spirits because paratroopers always get combat pay, even in peacetime, because of their dangerous duty. This enabled him to get his only son through the Chicago Medical University and to practice Medicine in Colorado. Medical doctors are very special and may be the object of Vic's survival.

Chapter Twenty-One

Exorcism

O ne day, a famous clairvoyant came to me, knowing that I was always writing when not working. "Let me tell you about an exorcism I attended with a Lutheran priest," she said, over the phone. I had never met her before; her husband had always brought their taxes to me. She recounted the circumstances where a young, professional male had been tormented physically and emotionally; felt pressured to jump out a window when he was home alone. He had been suicidal and very depressed over a broken relationship. She and a team of spiritualists, consisting of a priest and three female clairvoyants, had been called to visit the young man and help him in any way possible.

"When we got to his house, we had the man take a seat and the Lutheran priest went behind him to sprinkle Holy Water over him. There was no reaction, telling us that the evil spirits were not in the victim— they were elsewhere in the apartment. That being the case, it was best for us to first remove him from the evil environment. So, we had one of the spiritualists take him out for a snack while the rest of us continued with the exorcism."

"We went through the house, looking for drugs, hidden wires, tape-recorders, or any other notable objects that would tell us more about his background or his lifestyle—anything to help us hunt down the bad spirits. There was nothing important in the main living space. Aside from a bunch unfolded blankets and some well-used pillows on the couch, nothing really strange stood out except the refrigerator, which was full of candles. We checked his bedroom and found it barren. No bed or any other sign of life. It was then that we started putting the pieces together:"

"The blankets and pillows on the couch: The man had previously, moved out of his bedroom because he was being tormented by the spirits there."

"The candles: The man may have been attempting to utilize some form of witchcraft to bring about some form of revenge upon his departed lover."

"The barren bedroom: The attempt at a curse must have backfired and, rather than unleashing the wraiths onto his lover, the man only succeeded in releasing them into his own apartment.

"We placed a large expulsion-cross in the bedroom and an open Bible in the living space. We threw salt around the perimeter of the building. Then, we confiscated the candles and placed a blessing on the apartment before leaving."

"Shortly after, the man moved away to live with his family members and I don't blame him! Even if the house was exorcised, living all on your lonesome leaves you susceptible to all sorts of bad spirits—the worst demons are your own demons."

"I would know…," she said. She suddenly became silent and shivered as though a serpent were slithering up her back and hissing into her ears. Then, she took a deep breath, hardened her expression and continued. "When I got home from that exorcism, I felt haunted and this crushing feeling of negativity fell upon me. A few days later, my rosewood rosary—which I always kept in a box on my dresser— just disappeared. The day after that, I found it on my garage floor, torn apart, the beads scattered everywhere. Next was my Saint Christopher medal. I found it in the vacuum cleaner the following week when I emptied it into the trash. I started finding fine paper cuts on my hands and, even more frightening, on my daughter's hands in matching places. The same cuts appeared on both our knees as well."

Eventually, the happenings stopped but she had been utterly frightened. She told me that the effects of possession are like spider webs, often entangling other people who happen to come near the space of possession. She now fears exposure to the demons of the devil, so she no longer works on possession cases. It is clear that they are out there, just waiting for the opportunity to invade a person's spirit in times of weakness. There are good and bad spirits amongst us. Pray that the dark side does not get close enough to torment you and drag you into the throes of misery and suicide as with this man. Learn to keep away from people with spiritual problems and dark spirits. The clairvoyant who had interviewed over 400,000 individuals over the years, never took on another demon or possession case. She never heard about what ended up happening to the possessed, unfortunate man.

Later that year, the gifted clairvoyant was on the Women's TV Channel, in a month-long contest between psychics. She won the prize with ease. I don't envy her profession nor her gift to listen to everybody's fears and problems. I will stick to taxes for my time remaining. That is my present profession, solving my client's problems in the best way I know.

I remember when I was in a contentious relationship, on the cusps of leaving an influential and wealthy widow. We had a long heart-to-heart discussion one afternoon. When I visited the next morning, there were at least a hundred candles all over the house, which had burned down in the evening after I left. I never came back after that. Dark spirits are contagious, and I got as far away as I could. You need to think about these things as well and expose yourself to the light, not the darkness in the world.

This brings to mind a short story by Fyodor Dostoyevsky, "My Uncle's Dream". In the story, his uncle was a real sourpuss, always playing down everything and creating a real dark social atmosphere between himself and everybody he met. One night, he had a dream and dreamed that he had died and gone to heaven. Everybody in heaven was happy to be there and floated about in bliss. He started questioning the people he encountered regarding why they were so happy. There was no real answer and, after drifting through the heavens, the man found more people intently listening to his query and going away unhappy, like him. Eventually, everybody was unhappy, and he was his old self again, but heaven had changed from a state of bliss to a state of darkness because of him. When he woke up, he became a changed man. For the first time, he appreciated the good things in people and life around him. This is a lesson for all of us, that even the spirits need support, sooner or later and what goes around comes around.

Chapter Twenty-Two

Psychics

Clairvoyance—the ability to see into the future—has been with humanity since the dawn of history. The ancient Greeks had their Oracle of Delphi. Adolf Hitler surrounded himself with occultists, astrologers, and psychics who foretold of great events—one close psychic, who had predicted great happenings before the war, made the mistake of truthfully telling Adolph of his premonition of bad things to come, only a few days before the Army surrendered in Stalingrad, and was sent to the death camp for his advice. Big names, like Edgar Cayce and Nostradamus, are known to people across the world for their clairvoyant capabilities. But, perhaps, the most famous and renowned of all clairvoyants is Jesus who made prescient predictions regarding his own fate and that of his disciples.

Indian Chiefs and selected elders, such as Black Elk of the Sioux, who foresaw the Battle of Bighorn, were all revered and given important positions of high status. It seems that many important leaders had psychic abilities or a nearby psychic to advise them. Everybody values a person who gives good advice. A good psychic would generally not give bad advice unless coached in a way to suggest avoidance. Some psychics will play with the Tarot cards, but this is mostly to entertain clients as they can neither control nor influence the reading.

We are all a bit psychic. We intuitively sense when to avoid situations we don't feel good about, we can have dreams that become reality, and the more spiritual individuals will see and feel other people's vibrations. I am saying that if you can see or sense things in dreams or otherwise, you are psychic. You don't need to give readings for a living to be a psychic. It appears that we are all plugged into the same universe and the spiritual vibrations are everywhere.

My first encounter with a psychic was an African American woman who would scribble continuously with a pencil while she visited the spirits. Later she would do the same over the telephone. She seemed to be very good and I went to her after having heard of her from a referral, not an advertisement.

Once, I visited the Church of Tzaddi, a non-denominational church of different faiths. It was after working hours and I went with an employee because it was a really long drive to the church. The visitors for the session would go to the front of the room and leave a keepsake or house-keys on a table.

There were about twenty items on the table when the middle-aged lady entered. She went to the table without introduction and picked out a keyring. She handled it silently, for a minute, before beginning to speak about its owner. A young girl in the room gasped as she learned things about herself. Then, the psychic answered questions from the keyring's owner and moved on until she went through the whole pile of items. Near the end, she found the keys belonging to my employee and told her some things she didn't want to hear.

Finally, it was my turn. It seemed she was not predicting the future but, instead, was mostly tuned into the past and present enough to give some limited information about the object's bearer. It was truly amazing that she could connect the spiritual messages with nothing more than the items from the table. I had also left an item belonging to another lady in my office who couldn't attend in person. The psychic picked it up and identified her as a lady with short blonde hair who had three children. I asked the psychic if that was true because I knew she had only two pre-teen children. She affirmed her statement.

The next day at work, I told the blonde employee what the psychic had said. The lady turned white.

"Well, you only have two children, right?" I asked, jokingly. "No, I lost one at birth," was her reply.

There were other meetings with other people and, sometimes, I drew a blank. Other times, they were informative, but rarely do they provide true gems. One psychic (they all seem to be female) told me that I had missed my calling of being a writer. I hope this book will help disprove that statement. I was also told that I would be very unlucky with real estate (true), that I would be moving a lot (true), and that I would always be successful (true). Many visits I have forgotten, having no life-shattering or otherwise significant moments from what turned out to be more like entertainment than something useful. Except for one other.

Dawn M. was a professional psychic and would receive calls from a clearinghouse which billed the client's credit card for her time. At year-end, she would receive an income tax 1099-form and would need to see someone like me to account for her taxes, after expenses. I never met her because her husband would bring the forms and I would combine the two on their tax returns. I never thought much about it until I met up with her on one particular day.

She started to give me information that no ordinary person could have known. I learned that my Tax Court Appeal case was stuck because the real estate matter was being kicked around by the appeal auditors over its complexity. She said they would, ultimately, settle in my favor but that there was another element in the case that the client had not mentioned. This turned out to be an early withdrawal penalty for cashing in a pension, which would count against the client. Since this item was not contested, I still managed to win the case for the real estate matter. Her attention then shifted directly to me and she dismissed the book that I was writing at the time as going nowhere. It was never finished.

Another psychic visited my office after work, one day. Nothing she said made sense. This was to be a first and last visit until she mentioned something different.

"Who is Lady X?" she asked.

I thought for a minute and remembered a very sensual lady who had worked with me, a long time ago. "Just a lady I worked with many years ago. Why?"

She paused for a moment, flushed, and told me, "Well, she is thinking of you now and she likes you a lot. As a matter of fact, I am getting very uncomfortable and have to leave now." Then, she left with a coy smile and without another word. I realized, afterward, that the spirits must have been able to convey highly positive physical sensations as well as spiritual images.

There are many things floating around the universe which are available to those mediums who have the spiritual power to reach out and retrieve them for themselves or their clients, should that be the case. I believe many businessmen who rise to great power and wealth may well have a psychic edge about their next moves and opportunities. Spiritual matters are there for everybody.

Chapter Twenty-Three

Finding Elaine

I have a daughter named Elaine, after my beloved sister who died at age two. Elaine was always a sweet child but somewhat naïve. She would always hang out with classmates who were like her. Despite being given an abundance of love and attention, she always seemed to be out of focus during her school years and, later, with the difficult transition from child into the adult's social mainstream. She married but, after a long struggle, the marriage fell apart. Finally, she left sunny California for Wyoming in the dead of winter with a lazy loser boyfriend and her mind broke down. She had a complete mental and physical relapse from the stress of the poor marriage, her loser lazy druggie boyfriend, her endless work as a nurse's aide, and the intensely cold winter of places unknown.

On one especially cold day, not long afterward, I received a phone call from the local bus station. I was startled by the voice that I hadn't heard in nearly a year. It was my daughter—she and her three children had just arrived at the station and she asked if she could stay with us. The Social Services Department of a small town in Idaho, where they had drifted homeless, had bought them tickets to leave. We took her and the children in and found them an apartment a few months later.

Several years passed and the children grew up, flying through the school system. Two of them were exceptionally gifted; at age 13, one of them was already helping by running the computer for my practice. Their mother, on the other hand, continued to suffer from problems coping with life in general and was finally put into a state-run board and care. She would call weekly and I would visit her twice a month, a long drive through traffic since she was fifty miles from where I lived.

The years passed, and the children grew up, but their mother stayed at the supervised board and care. They gave her lots of freedom to wander around town and to receive visitors. She was considered "harmless and helpless". While she lived in a place that does not impart memories worth recalling, Elaine's mind was always off in space, somewhere far beyond the rest of us.

Last year, one of her gifted daughters who had married a successful software engineer, took Elaine under her wing for supervision and moved her to another institution near her residence—a hundred miles from me, in Pasadena. A week later, Elaine disappeared. She had wandered off with not the slightest recollection of her new home. Then, the ordeal began for the family. We rallied around the problem with busy phone calls to all the agencies and newspapers they could contact in Southern California. Pictures of her were copied and made into MISSING posters. The posters were sent to hospitals, police stations, the FBI, sheriffs, and the Salvation Army. Then, the waiting began.

Days passed with no word of Elaine. All the time, the family was seeking out new places to send picture posters and their phones were busy nonstop, calling and looking for possible signs of Elaine. The days turned into a week. My missing daughter had no real-world memory of anything but a few phone numbers. But the phone didn't ring at all. She was without identification, money, or anything on her person. We were convinced she would turn up dead or was lost in the sea of the homeless in Los Angeles.

Suddenly, there was a welcomed call from the Seventh Day Adventist Hospital in East Los Angeles. Elaine had wandered in the day before, off the street. She was dehydrated, hungry, suffering from exposure, and exhausted. She had told the hospital personnel at the emergency room that her name was "Clinton". They kept her overnight and improved her physical condition enough to discharge her.

Since she had no address or home to speak of, they were going to turn her loose on the street outside when a nurse remembered seeing her picture somewhere. The nurse could not remember where she saw her because Elaine's picture was seen on Facebook, Posters, and the local news. The persistent nurse called several agencies before finding her identity. That nurse's profoundly simple act of compassion probably saved Elaine's life. God Bless her.

Now, she is back in the new board and care facility, and visits at family gatherings. She has no memory of what had happened to her, where she had been, whether she had eaten or drank anything for the duration of that week, and no recollection of how she had traveled the 75 miles journey from the board and care to the hospital. She does not remember how she had fed herself or where she had slept. Authorities told us that homeless people are allowed to travel on buses free sometimes in the LA Area and the drivers are usually helpful. Outside of that, her whole week is a complete blank. Curiosity and concern aside, we are all happy to have her back and to have her safe. My phone rings weekly from her welcomed call and there is always something we can do for her. I still think of her as my little girl as if she went away a long time ago. I know the etheric spirits were taking care of Elaine and that they guided her safely to the hospital where the observant godsent nurse saved her from an unknown but unthinkable future out on the streets. God blessed everybody involved.

Chapter Twenty-Four

Circle of Life

Most of humanity's spiritual messages draw their most basic elements from a common conceptual origin found deep within the ether. These thought-provoking ideas drift around, freely and aimlessly, until they come upon a person of interest—a person whose mind is open and free to absorb the messages—and materialize in their consciousness.

One of these concepts is that of a "Tree of Life" which appears in almost all religions and cultures. In the Bible, the Tree is present in the Old Testament as the apple tree bearing the forbidden fruit of knowledge of good and evil. Before eating the fruit of that tree, Adam and Eve lived in the Garden of Eden, a material paradise devoid of need, suffering, and death. It was only after consuming from the tree that the concept of death was introduced to humanity. Now, one might interpret this to imply that the tree was a "Tree of Death" rather than the "Tree of Life", but I disagree. Life and death are two sides of the same coin, a yang and a yin bound in an eternal dance—an eternal cycle of change. A life without death, a life without change, isn't really a "life" at all: it is simply "existing". Yes, partaking of the fruit of the tree brought the inevitability of death to Adam and Eve; however, in doing so, it also allowed them to truly "live" for the first time—to leave a mark upon the world by living a life beyond endless wallowing in an unthinking paradise.

In American Sioux Indian culture, the tree represents the tribe's life and future as illustrated by Black Elk's Great Vision of a vibrant tree that stood as the center of Life in their Nation's Circle. The local Pechanga Indians refer to their Tree of Life as the eternal strength and durability of their tribe as represented by the over 1,000-year-old Oak which had, for generations, provided acorns to sustain the tribe. This sacred tree is unlike any other. Its massive branches all bend down to reach the ground; as an umbrella searching supports, they travel over the ground, thick as tree trunks, and appear again, to rise and leaf as though they were individual trees. They also provide huge support for the shortened master trunk and provide a gigantic open canopy with shelter underneath. It is a sight to behold but is now off limits as a sacred site for the Pechanga tribe.

I wrote the *Metric Clock*, my story about a nine-year-old child, many years ago. The book is about time, how a year in the boy's life is broken into seasons, and about the child imagining a clock of 100 minutes instead of 60. While I wrote it, I had another, the inevitability vision—one of the Wheel of Life.

"The thoughts that came to me were about the Metric 100- minute Clock of 25, 50, 75, and 100 minutes increments, but with only one hand. This hand started turning slowly clockwise from the 100-minute top and changed into a baby. The baby waved his arms up and down. As the hand progressed to the right quarter the baby changed into a small boy. The boy smiled as he grew. Then, he proceeded to grow tall and thin as a young man. The hand kept moving down and the young man grew older and heavier. The look on

his face became very serious and concerned. When the hand moved into the final quarter, he was much older with pure white hair. Pain was evident in his features. The hand kept moving until the fragile man suddenly appeared lifeless. The hand stopped at 100, and then it began to turn again. The baby was there as before with different clothes, but his face and movement were the same. Charles began to recognize the child in the clock. It was the same child in the pictures that his mother had taken of him with the Kodak Brownie camera. Then, he woke up—wide-eyed, staring at the ceiling of his little bedroom."

Years later, when I read "Black Elk Speaks" by John Neihardt, I read about the same Wheel of Life as it was described by the Sioux prophet. The same vision had come to me while I was writing the story about the child who happened to be the same age that the Indian boy, Black Elk, had in his Great Vision. Black Elk's vision went from old man, the Sixth Grandfather of wisdom, the Spirit of the Earth, to a young child. This pointed to the same direction as my vision. This is proof that some thoughts are omnipresent, as surely as some statements are codified by the Bible or passed down in stone or prayer or pictographs from generations as the generational histories of tribal mankind, for we are all tribes. They are universal and a natural part of mankind as we share space on this earth together. It is certainly an eternal Wheel of Life to show our worldly growth and experience. Open your mind and soul to let the spirits prevail in our guidance and lives.

Riverside, California is home to the Sherman Indian School where Hopi and Navajo Indian children were brought off the reservation and housed there to be educated and find a place in this white man's world. One of their teachers was a small Navajo named Harry Gus, my only client with two first names. For many years he and his Hopi wife visited as clients and close friends. Eventually, I joined the local Indian Council, a small non-profit for all Indians in the area which also included Apaches. The Indians would visit the reservations and bring back woven beautiful tapestries and artifacts to sell to me because the Trading Posts paid very little for them. They would talk of a place where they could see all the stars, and experience nature without civilization. I still have the tapestries, one of which is on the cover of this book.

Early one morning, an elderly Navajo lady visited me. "My grandbaby died, and I need money to bury her," she confided solemnly, tears welling up in her eyes. I wrote her a check and she gave me her treasured heirloom silver squash blossom necklace (see *Figure 1*). I told her I would keep it forever because it was very special, and I still have it. It was probably the only asset this lady possessed because they were people with simple wants and needs.

Later on, one of the Council members stole money from me. He was an independent contractor and I paid him for a job which he never showed up to do. I asked other members of the Council what they would do about it. "Nothing," they said. "He is one of us." That was when I quit the Board because nobody can be effective when working with thieves. Two years later, the Council disbanded and disappeared. I was sorry to see them go because they were very nice people.

Harry retired and would visit my office several times a year with his crude guitar. He would play and sing an Indian song for me in Navajo. I would always welcome him or his son, Larry, a free-spirited kid with long black shoulder length hair, who would never work but independently traveled all over the country to photograph Indian events and the Wounded Knee Massacre Remembrance. Harry had never mentioned his military experience and I never connected him with the Army, but he was there in WWII. He served as a Code Talker which was a Navajo communication system to confuse the Japanese who would splice into our com lines and pick up conversations. At his military funeral, his eulogy also noted that he was in the Aleutians where the fighting was, and he thought he would die from the extreme cold and terrible conditions. He didn't mention it, but the Army didn't issue cold weather clothes and gear for the winter campaign.

I believe the GI Educational Bill put him through college afterward, so he could teach his people to cope with our civilization. I still miss Harry and his family, but I have things in my office to remind me of his culture and the warm simplicity of Indian spiritual life. I used my Native American Navajo ceremonial Tree of Life tapestry as the cover of this book because I felt it was so wonderfully spiritual. It speaks for itself. I have also enclosed copies of some of my Native American collection in this chapter. They are too beautiful to reside in a dark cabinet.

We should keep in mind that the Native Indians considered all things sacred. The mindless slaughter of their buffalo was incomprehensible to people who considered all things holy and that everything, as in our own Old Testament, that which comes from the Earth, goes back to the Earth. That is why it is referred to as the Mother Earth. In the classic movie, *The Treasure of Sierra Madre*, after the miners took all the gold out of the mountain that it had to give, the old miner told his fellow miners,

"Don't be in such a hurry to leave. The mountain has given up her treasure. We have wounded her and must repair and clean up the mine the best we can before we go." John Houston was certainly a man of all times because we live in an era of short-term gains, at a cost of long-term losses.

Figure 1: The Zuni heirloom silver Squash-Blossom necklace.

Figure 2: A striped lightning pattern Navajo tapestry. It was given to me from the Reservation.

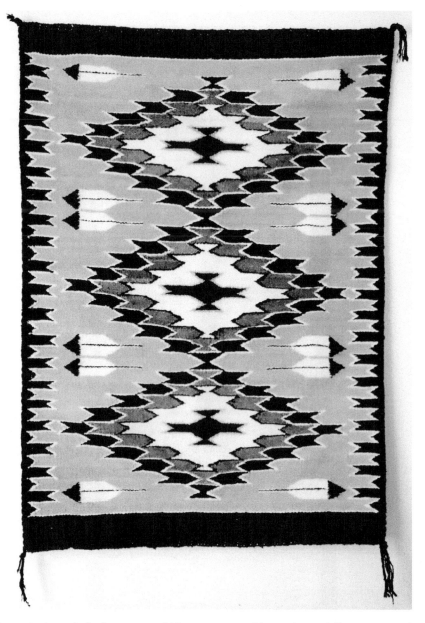

Figure 3: An eagle-feather-patterned Navajo tapestry. Obtained on a different occasion but at the same Reservation.

Figure 4: A diamond-back snakeskin-patterned Navajo tapestry. Received as a gift. These are all made of natural wool and dyes—they can't be washed normally.

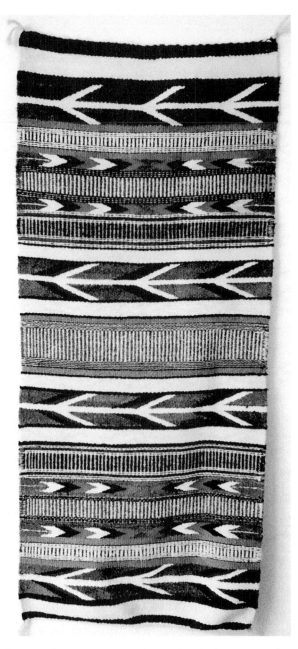

Figure 5: Another striped Navajo tapestry, this one has feather patterns for an assortment of different birds.

Figure 6: Another striped Navajo tapestry.

Figure 7: A collection of Native American obsidian tools and weapons. The larger piece in the center is likely a scraper. It is surrounded by arrowheads of various sizes and a spearhead on the lower-right corner.

Figure 8: A Navajo cottonwood and raw-hide drum.

Figure 9: A native American Flute made by Steve "Three Feathers" Meiers a retired school teacher

Figure 10: Davy Crockett Mk-54 This low-yield plutonium nuclear rocket was reconfigured to be carried in a backpack in Chapter 20 Suicide Bomber by an Airborne Soldier

Chapter Twenty-Five

Combat Pay in The Cold War

Sometimes, things are not what they appear to be and, by default, they can be the opposite of the perception. Soldiers of our Potemkin Army of 1957 beware: let the spirits guard and watch over us.

I enlisted at 18 and was aware, like most other young enlistees, that there was a draft. That meant that, sooner or later, you would be called up. However, no one was afraid of that at the time. The real motivation for enlisting was to get away from home and find some adventure in life. Besides, because of my high-test scores (mental-physical: 1-A), I qualified for every Army school in the brown book, including Officers Candidate School. I had enlisted in the Explosives Ordinance Disposal Service because it looked like a fun job and paid $55 per month in combat pay in addition to the lavish $100 for the 5½ day and night week. Then, I was talked into signing it away for the O.C.S. and combat arms training at Fort Chaffee, Arkansas, where I would be trained on 105-MM (four-inch) howitzers and have my name emblazoned in gold on my helmet.

A month into the program, I was called into a meeting where an officer asked, "Do you have a college degree?"

"No, Sir. I am only 18 and just out of high school."

"Well, then," the officer mused, a weary hint of annoyance in his tone,

"You are no longer an OCS candidate because the new requirements are for a college degree." And, with that statement, they took a piece of scotch tape and eliminated my golden name. A year later, I would take an all-day test and get a worthless freshman year credit from the University of Maryland for them. Once a soldier had enlisted, or been drafted after basic training, he had no options of other schools unless he reenlisted, so I was stuck for another 2 ½ years.

I had been shorted out from my original school by the O.C.S. fiasco and the only interesting option available was Airborne Artillery where they jumped with the hardware. I had decided to go for the combat pay again and signed up for the Airborne, ending up at Fort Bragg, North Carolina. Jump school was hard and I survived my classes to lose my helmet on my first jump when I hit the blast behind the inboard engine of the C-130 Lockheed Hercules. After my fifth jump, I received my wings.

I would have remained gung-ho, but my spirits were cut short by a belligerent egomaniac, sadistic, Master Sergeant who called himself War Daddy Therriac. The entirety of his career seemed to revolve around terrorizing and harassing young recruits. He disliked my buddy Cosby and ordered him to run around the barracks every night with a full field pack until one day, he couldn't take it anymore and went AWOL. Every day, Captain Rice would look me up and tell me that the boy's father was calling him and asking where his boy was. The captain would ask me if I knew where he went, and I honestly told him I had no idea at all. The boy turned himself in, a week later, after having worked as a dishwasher in a restaurant not far away. Cosby was a very nice and intelligent recruit who should have been in college instead of the Army. For his suffering, and despite receiving paratrooper wings, he received a dishonorable discharge which ruined parts of his future. Wardaddy also had me in his sights, but I managed to transfer out of the company and into a nuclear rocket company with better management.

I was assigned to drive a major all over Fort Campbell, Kentucky in an annual event where, this year, the 82nd would invade the 101st at Campbell and, the next year, the 101st would invade Fort Bragg. The major, a nice fellow from Division named Lapke, was an observer who was only there to note problems or successes with the airborne drop of equipment before the troops landed in the drop zone. I was driving a jeep covered in flags over the dirt roads to the Drop Zone when a jet fighter plane came over us from out of nowhere, on our right side, and blasted us off the road with his sonic afterburner. "That was the 'You're dead' welcome to Campbell," the major remarked with a grin as we got the jeep back on the road.

At the drop zone, the heavy drop started on schedule as the trucks, trailers, and guns slid out the backs of the C-130 transports. They came down very fast, each with three huge parachutes to slow their descent. Maybe the lead pilot ignored the pathfinder's flares, or the wind changed, but the deuce-and-a-half trucks and equipment began landing closer and closer to us on our side of the drop zone.

Then, one came right towards us and everybody began panicking. We couldn't tell where it was going to land, but we knew it would be close. Our knot of a half-dozen observers looked upward as a truck on a platform sailed overhead and bounced three feet in the air as it landed, safely, next to us. Everybody looked at each other in amazement and began taking notes without saying a word. The Spirits were certainly helpful that day to save all of us from being squashed like a bug on the sands of Fort Campbell. For three minutes, our lives hung in the balance and we had no control over our fate. We saw it coming but stood our ground like a target on the shooting range waiting for that random bullseye.

The next time a trooper was almost killed was in the skies over Germany. We were jumping from C-130s when the trooper in front of me went out the door and got caught up in the static lines hanging out the side of the door. The parachutes were hooked on a steel cable in the plane so, when you went out the door, the bag containing the parachute pulls away, thus opening the canopy from the propeller and exhaust blast of the engines. Alex had gotten trapped in the thicket of bags from other jumpers. For a nerve-wracking half-hour, the trooper hung near the tail of the plane, the lines taut around his neck. The panicked jumpmaster and Air Force NCO slowed the plane down and attempted to pull him back in. There was no sign if he had been strangled, or was unconscious, or alive. Nothing they tried worked because the propeller blast kept pushing against him. The pilots were afraid to land because he would become hamburger on the runway. The remaining option would be to cut his static line.

Suddenly, the trooper freed himself from the knot of bags and lines and his chute opened to safely slow his fall to Earth. He landed in a German farmer's field, his neck and uniform all bloody. The farmer proceeded to curse and admonish him for trespassing while chasing the poor trooper off his land. What was important, however, was that he survived despite the odds. I was the next man on the stick and might not have survived in his position. He had the Spirits or Guardian watching over him that day. Such is our fate.

On a NATO C-130 jump over France, near the Pyrenees Mountains, I experienced a "Mae West" malfunction. There are two major ways to get killed in a jump. One is a streamer malfunction where the chute doesn't catch the airplane engine blast and streams overhead like a sheet, without opening. We were jumping at 1,250-feet altitude and a person would normally fall at 35 feet per second for about three seconds before the air resistance would level off to a 100- fps fall. The trooper would have about 15-seconds to live after going out the door. The other way to get killed is to have the "Mae West" malfunction—when the riser lines connecting the edges of the parachute to the trooper's harness cross over the top of the chute. This forms a big bra shape that doubles the fall speed because the canopy is compromised by the air going around it. A trooper dealing with this has a quarter minute to fall to his death.

I jumped and after the blast, and I remember checking my canopy and finding my risers stuck in the middle of the chute. I was falling very fast. I realized the predicament I was in but was too caught up in the shock to do anything about it. The seconds ticked past and the wind howled in my ears as I plummeted. Suddenly, I noticed the risers begin to roll over one side of my chute, one after the other. The thought of pulling my reserve, which could have saved me, or been caught in the chute and killed me, completely eluded me as I was enraptured by the sight. One by one, the lines slid away from the middle until the chute popped open, barely far enough above the ground. It slowed me, and I hit the ground really hard, tearing my field jacket. I lay on the ground for a minute with my chute pulling on me from the breeze, shaken from the hard landing, and dazzled by the experience. Then, I got up and fol-lowed the troopers to the trucks outside the DZ. I always jumped with a camera in my canteen case and had my picture taken—pictures that I still have today. This was a gift from my spiritual guardian. Never do people survive a "Mae West" malfunction and live to tell the tale. In all of my 21 jumping experiences, I had never seen this malfunction or even a streamer, and I realized how fortunate I was to have been saved by the spirits. At the time, I just thought I was lucky. Years later, I realized that there was a reason for my having hung around so long on this earth. That amazing experience concluded my military tour.

For a month, my outfit was consigned to assist and help pack parachutes with the packers in a fighter Luftwaffe airbase at Augsburg, Germany. Our unit living quarters were the German fighter pilots' wartime private rooms, complete with beds and dressers—a great increase in modesty from the 40-double stacked at our barracks back in Baumholder. Above the long tables in the hangar where the parachutes were stretched out, there was a heavy roof supporting. On one place in the beam, there was a huge dent where a bomb, during the World War, had hit without exploding. Had the bomb exploded the hanger would not have been there.

After a few weeks, the cooks who I had befriended came to me and said, "We're going to Salzburg, Austria for the weekend. Would you like to come along?"

"Sure," I replied, "But that is another country and my pass is only good for Augsburg."

"No problem. We will put it in the mess hall typewriter and add Salzburg after Augsburg."

That weekend we went to the ancient capital of the Habsburg Empire where the old castle dominates the city. In the city where Mozart was born, I encountered a lady at a guesthouse and spent my time at her place, looking pleasantly out her window to a meadow and the Alps beyond. Sunday came quickly and, in the twilight, I caught a bus to meet with the cooks and their Opel at a guesthouse next to the autobahn. After leaving the bus, I couldn't find the bar on the autobahn. I was perplexed and totally lost. I panicked. If I didn't get back to Augsburg, I would go to jail for going AWOL and for desertion. I stood under a streetlight with distress and sweat pouring out of every pore in my body when a young Austrian came by on a motorcycle. He stopped, and his rider slid off the back seat. "What's wrong?" he asked, in very good English.

"I'm supposed to meet my buddies at a bar on the autobahn to get back to Augsburg and I have no idea where I am."

"You are on the wrong side of town. There are two autobahns here." He then spoke to his passenger in German. "Here, jump on the back seat and I will take you there."

I got behind him, thanking him profusely, and we buzzed across town in ten minutes. We found my buddies standing impatiently in front of the guesthouse on the autobahn. I thanked my biker again and he happily left after delivering his good deed. My buddies had been waiting quite a while for me and drove off as soon as I arrived. We arrived that evening in good spirits and I tucked into my little Luftwaffe pilot's bed, still assessing my circumstances. Who sent the kind Austrian? Why was I so lucky? What would have happened to me if I hadn't met my buddies before they left town? Only my spirit guardian could answer these questions. Like the bomb that failed to explode in the hanger, there were spirit friends available to save me whenever I was in a bad corner. I was blessed with a good guardian.

During my three years with the military, we were supposed to be the elite units before the Vietnam War. The cadre treated us like dogs and would summarily order us to nighttime punishment duty for crimes such as looking away or down when they passed. The officers practiced, "Yes, Sir" and "No, Sir" as conversational "we don't want to know or hear from you" English. We were a name tag and number, never to be known otherwise. We called ourselves cannonballs because we were expendable, even though every outfit I was in was at half-strength because of a lack of reenlistments. My outfit in Germany included dozens of ordinary soldiers who couldn't jump because the company strength fell below 50% which is non-functional and brought them in to fill the ranks. We were not allowed to wear our airborne wings on our fatigues. They also deducted salaries for German KPS (German Civilian Kitchen Workers) under the ruse that they were doing our jobs. This was in addition to mandatory $50 deductions from our monthly paychecks.

The Germans proudly called their airborne troops "Fallschirm Yeager's" which means parachute hunters. We were parachute expendables without any glorious names or treatment. We were awfully glad to go home and see our families, the big collie, and friends again after leaving The War, as we called it. The Army was at war with itself. I did not sign up for active reserves and, when the Vietnam War started up three years later, I was not called in. If I had stayed in Explosives Ordinance Disposal, I would have been the first to be called in and probably would have been blown up. If I had gone to OCS, I would have been involved as a professional junior officer and also subject to frontline combat. My MOS as a cannonball led me to a non-essential role which labeled me as "not worth calling back in". Yet, I was the only man in my company who achieved a direct hit on a moving tank target in the battery exercise with the 105MM howitzers. Thank God for the spirits that looked after me for my tour of duty and protecting me afterward from Nam where 10% of the combatants were killed and 15% or more were wounded for a score of 25 % of all combat troops. I went into the military a boy and left as a man. My personal motto is: "Always in harm's way but still here afterward". But I did have a lot of help from the spirits around me.

Daniel Schmittner, another close friend, after the three years of harassment, went home to California and committed suicide a year later. His spirits let him go to a better place. Unfortunately, it was his time, at only 22. I still think of Dan, now and again. He was a highly intelligent fellow and I remember him, working out in the rock pile behind our barracks one evening after an enemy NCO overheard him say the dreaded word 'cannonball' in the squad bay. Three years of harassment ended the life of this highly intelligent sensitive person.

———

There were few good times in the peacetime Cold War Army. We were on combat alert at all times but needed to participate in Divisional training jumps every three months or lose our combat pay. We needed to travel from our Baumholder NATO mountain camp many miles to Wiesbaden Air Base at the Main River. The weather would frequently change from fair to stormy which would be too windy to jump and we would need to turn the whole convoy around and return. On one trip we were on the three month edge of losing jump pay when we arrived at the tarmac where a C-130 Lockheed Hercules was waiting, but there were no parachutes for us. After some heated discussions between two company commanders, an infantry company of the 504 Regiment took their chutes off and gave them to us for the jump. Between communications disasters and the bad weather delays a decision was made to make most of our jumps at a forest clearing in the camp hills where we were stationed.

The Baumholder airbase was incredibly small and housed only small single engine planes for scouting and surveillance and a few larger single engine Canadian DE Haviland Otter cargo planes which had D rings for tie-downs inside instead of web seats and static lines. It was much closer and we would get up at three in the morning instead of one or two for the trip to Wiesbaden. Officer's wives would gather around the drop zone between the hills to watch us come down with many of us including their husbands, landing in the trees nearby. One day a trooper caught an up drafted current which carried him off to a nearby town with the company jeep in hot pursuit. I am sure that there are photos on the walls of some officers dormitories after the wives snapped a picture or two of their mates hanging from trees. I know, because I have some.

———

Elvis Presley was drafted for two years and, after basic training, sent to Germany in 1979. He made a deal, which was much publicized, to avoid the Special Services which was the Army Musical Corps, and serve as an ordinary soldier doing his duty. His singing career was put on hold. The tour of duty was not particularly ordinary as he was made a sergeant and assigned as a jeep driver for an Armored Division Headquarters Commander, Colonel Parker. I met one of the tankers who gave me the whole story. As you know, there are no secrets in the Army. Elvis lived off base with his father and had a very easy life. The only problem was that he would fight with his father over the choice of the women knocking on the door after hours. He got along fine with his commander Colonel Parker, and lots of freedom, Colonel Parker would change careers later on to become the agent for Elvis when the tour of duty was completed stateside.

Life can be good for our favorites.

Chapter Twenty-Six

The Curse

I believe that most problems in life are inherited from Karma. Otherwise, why would innocent people be murdered? Why would genocide be committed? The Buddhist karmic cycle explains that we are reincarnated repeatedly until we have overcome our flaws and the sins of our past lives. Accordingly, a person would be born mutilated in this life to offset his crime of mutilating someone in the past. I have already covered some examples of that with myself and with my wife. I do believe that we not only learn to be adults by going through all the trials and tribulations of young adulthood but learn to grow away from our present life shortcomings and mature to correct them and become a more perfect person. Thus, we experience a living karmic progression beyond what we have inherited.

A client, John, was a manager of an apartment building. He was an ordinary person who had emigrated from Wales, a part of Great Britain, as my own people did from Scotland and England, over three hundred years ago. He would repair plumbing, paint vacant units, and keep the place in good order in lieu of rent for himself and his wife. I had known the man for many years and we were great friends, always glad to see each other annually. John had kept a small retail clothing business out of town which had faded away when the business diminished. I had not seen him in ten years when, suddenly, he reappeared in my life.

John had been a Good Samaritan to the people in the apartment house, always helping people when he could and enjoying his work. One of the renters was a single, retired, medical doctor named Morton who had few, if any, friends. The elderly man leaned on John to help run errands and assist him more and more over the years as he slowed down and needed help and companionship. Morton never disclosed his past to John except that he had been a medical doctor-psychiatrist at the State institution in Patton, California. Over the years, he learned to trust John with all his affairs and made John his executor and heir to part of his estate. John came to visit me several times over Morton's investment paperwork and again when he needed estate work done for the good doctor. It was good to meet up with John again and I got to know his wife and her lawyer relatives. The good doctor, Morton, passed away and, while we were reviewing Morton's estate, John found a very long handwritten letter that the doctor had left behind.

The letter had been written to explain Morton's life as a doctor. There were tears shed reading it. He had struggled, as all medical students do, to get through medical school. Not only is it demanding, but the intelligence level of a medical doctor is exactly the same as for a military general—an average IQ of 125—which is the top five percent of the population. Deprived of normal social life and a working wage, he was interned in a large prestigious hospital in New England, near where he had gone to medical school. His whole life and future, he explained in writing to his unknown heirs, was based on his success in the emergency rooms of his internship with doctor mentors noting everything he did.

At one point, he dated a senior doctor's daughter. An otherwise normal relationship quickly grew into a nightmare. Morton, according to his missive, did nothing improper outside of an innocent kiss. It may have been more, however, and the young lady complained to her parents, and especially her father, who became irate. The senior doctor complained to his medical intern team whom John practiced with and tore into Morton, forcing him to change mentors. The girl's father was determined to mercilessly impugn Morton in the hospital, in his career, and in his life. Morton was cursed in the worst way.

After Morton graduated from his internship, he found a promising position in another hospital. Shortly afterward, he was terminated, without justifiable cause, based on rumors from the old internship. Time after time, even after moving out of state, he would be pursued by that curse and lost position after position, not by his work, but by the curse from his internship mentor. Finally, although his specialty was not psychiatry, he was able to acquire a position with a small mental hospital for the criminally insane in Southern California. He was now a state employee and was able to get tenure and gain relief from the curse. But, he never really escaped. He had never intended to be a psychiatrist or medical doctor for the insane. He had only managed to grasp onto a job that nobody wanted.

Morton spent the rest of his life waking up every day as a single man, not wanting to be exposed to female companionship, and living with the curse of his life and career. He was able to write some defining articles about treatment of the mentally insane and win awards for his practice, but never had a normal productive personal social life afterward.

The lesson here is to be careful with your actions. Everything you do can affect others and can, ultimately, lead to the destruction of your own life. We might all, one day, find ourselves trapped by a single event—courtesy of the karma that we've created for ourselves. So, we must be fortunate or wise enough to keep out of trouble's way. No need to look for trouble when, sooner or later, it may come looking for you. The young girl in Dr. Morton's date may have simply been overly sensitive about his romantic notions and given the wrong message to her father. Regardless, there was no guardian or spirit to guide this talented but unfortunate man through his lifetime and, falling victim to the karma of his actions, he ended up where he didn't want to be; all alone, cursed to spend his life contemplating his fate. On the other hand, because of the curse, the mental hospital received the services of a very gifted and loyal physician.

Chapter Twenty-Seven

Farewell

When I was a child, I had a great imagination. Even though the nearest trains were miles away, on the other side of town, I saw trains thundering down the street on hundreds of huge wheels screeching against steel rails as the sharp call of its whistle filled the air through the eyes of my mind. Once, I saw a fishing port on the marsh road that ran between the hills and the swampy marsh. The rivers of seawater would rush in with the tide and fill the channels of mucky, polluted, black, slimy residue. I was so convinced that an older neighbor friend Tony, who swore that nothing was there, pedaled down there with me on his handlebars. And, of course, there was nothing to be found except my embarrassment. Many years later Tony, who kept pigeons in his garage attic, would graduate at Harvard with a doctorate in Biology.

A neighbor-client of 30 years, both husband and wife college professors, used to visit my offices annually and I would welcome them as old friends. When we moved our offices from our Walnut residence to Temecula and they faithfully followed each year, even staying in local hotels the night before to break the drive of the round trip. Several years ago, they told me that they wouldn't be able to make the trip again—this year would be the last year. Edison C. began to recite a Browning sonnet from memory. It took ten minutes and, every time he got hung up, his wife Nenita, would fill in the missing words. There were tears in my eyes afterward. I never saw them again, but we still exchange Christmas Cards.

An elderly client, whose husband had passed away several years before, was having difficulty navigating her way into our offices. After she settled down, we completed her interview and she made a statement:

"This is the last year that I'll be coming here. The doctors have given me less than six months to live."

Tears crept into my eyes. She had been a client for decades and I had always looked forward to her visits. "Have you made your peace with your Maker?" I asked her, in sympathy.

"Yes," she proudly answered, "I made my peace years ago." Then, she left, not fearful at all of her future. She was at peace with the universe, the spirits, and herself.

A new client, Ann T. came in this year to file a joint return without her husband who was absent because of work. She told me that she only had six months to live because of cancer. She usually did their taxes herself, because they were not complicated, but came to me this year because she wanted her husband to have a place to come next year when she was gone. He would not be capable of doing their taxes as she had and so she was establishing as many contacts as possible before her time was up. I believe this is the most unselfish act I had ever experienced with a client. This was true love.

A little French lady had lost her husband a year before and now it was her turn to say goodbye. She had met him in France during WWII and they married afterward.

"I have a serious heart problem and my doctors tell me that I will not be around for another visit. I have always liked coming here and will miss you. Now, I will tell you my secret," she said smiling inside, "My husband and I lived apart, these past few years. We had two houses and he stayed in the one with his seventy cats."

I was incredulous. "Seventy cats?"

"Yes," she laughed, jovially. "It was a real mess to clean up." And with that, she left with a smile, taking her secret with her forever.

An elderly client had come to me for many years. One year, Al told me why he was alone. "At breakfast one morning, my wife was sitting across from me and she said, 'I don't feel good'. Before I could ask her what was wrong she fell over dead." He sighed, "It was a complete surprise and I have been alone ever since." Our demise can be sudden but without hardly any pain or farewell.

Walter S. had entered his Alzheimer's affected wife into a nursing home. The client was always joking and carrying about. This made him one of my favorite clients because he had such a disarming sense of humor. The year before, he had a story about how difficult it was to remove a water tower behind his house when they discovered it was full of sand instead of water. I had found out that his wife had died, from the family, and offered my condolences. The client accepted my empathy and decided to fill in some of the facts.

"She escaped from the nursing home—went through the front door when nobody was looking. Probably one of her saner moments. She was always trying to get home, you see? Before they realized that she was missing, she was run over by a train that passed behind the building." He paused, and a wicked smile creased his face. "She always liked trains, though."

My mother had died of Alzheimer's and it is terrible to be separated from one's family in such a time of need and comfort. Though the irony was apparent, I failed to feel his humor at that moment.

A neighbor invited my wife and me to visit his church and, for many Sundays afterward, we attended mass with him and his wife. The retired couple were both devoted Christians. One day, he commented that he wished he was dead.

"Why?" I asked, appalled. I knew that he and his wife were inseparable and always had been, throughout their long lives.

"Because," he explained, a sense of longing tinged in his voice, "I can go to heaven and meet Christ and the Disciples."

"But what about your wife? You would leave her here to go to heaven?"

"Yes, I would leave her here to go to heaven because it is better there than earth," he responded easily. To him, it was a matter of fact.

"But, I thought Christ said heaven was on Earth."

"No," he replied. Then, he stood to conclude our conversation and affirm his belief, "It is better up there."

I never could believe this man or any other would leave their family behind simply because heaven was supposed to be better than Earth. Why not pass away in regular time, as we all will, and then see what it is about?

Ecclesiastes said, *"He who is joined with all the living has hope, for a living dog is better than a dead lion"*. He also said, *"Enjoy life with the wife whom you love, all the days of your vain life that He has given you under the sun because that is your portion in life and in your toil at which you toil under the sun."*

Some people never get to say farewell. The mother of a Danish-born associate accountant who I worked with, many years ago, was one such person. The accountant was a very smart and likable person. His family in Denmark was dominated by his high-flying flashy brother who dealt in large-scale investment deals. One deal in particular involved building a resort on the Spanish Mediterranean coast. The resort was never completed and many investors lost money on the project. An unhappy investor visited the family's home and shot my associates' unsuspecting mother to death, through a window. For many people, money is more important than a person's life and the poor woman paid the price for a bad investment. For reasons unknown, her investment-advisor son wasn't home that day and escaped the fate intended for him.

Sometimes, there is no guardian spirit to save the innocent. Karma could be at fault, but fate and causality can be related here without reason.

A seasoned police detective once told me that, in most murder crimes, money or women is the cause—often both at once.

There was a seasonal tax interviewer who dabbled in real estate investment matters. By the end of the first year working with him, he moved out of town, but his problems followed him wherever he went. My office received a death-wish Christmas card addressed to him from an unhappy investor. We reap what we sow.

The Chinese attribute success to good luck. Although I will acknowledge that good fortune is a powerful factor, I believe that success involves far more than a simple dice-roll. Success is manufactured by hard work and good habits. An example:

A client of many years was a man about town. Glenn S. had moved to Palm Springs and, being sociable and impeccably dressed, he quickly got to know everybody there. He engaged in conversation with everybody he met, accumulated a vast list of friends and, because he was tall and handsome, had many girlfriends. He was a traveling consultant for several Japanese auto manufacturers and would visit their dealerships all over the country to instruct the workers on how to do things the company's way. He was a professional in public relations.

One day, he brought a new girlfriend to my office. This was nothing new—I had already met all his present and past wives who had come with him for his taxes. This lady was much younger than him and was very pretty. Based on the way she carried herself, she was used to getting her way. Glenn introduced her to me and it turned out that she was the granddaughter of a wealthy royal family that had been exiled from the mid-eastern oil-bearing states. As was her custom, she voluntarily tried to haggle the tax preparation fee down, to no avail and to my client's annoyance. They left hand in hand and he helped her into the old used Rolls Royce he had bought to please her.

Later, at year-end, he called about a business matter and, in our casual conversation, revealed that he had left her. "It just didn't work out because she is too independent for me." I chuckled, thinking that was the extent of his reasoning, but he continued.

"Let me tell you what actually happened. I was driving down Palm Springs Blvd. when her chauffeur came by, in the empty limousine, and motioned for me to pull over. I stopped my old Corvette and went to his window when he nervously told me that the girl had put out a hit on me. The man was perfectly serious and because he liked me, he was giving me fair warning that she was on the warpath. I walked away, shaking like a leaf, but made it to a nearby phone booth. I called all of the members of her family that I knew and, finally, managed to get the hit called off."

My friend survived that relationship because everywhere he goes, he creates friends and connections. In this case, that probably saved his life. He is now retired and lives with his fourth wife in Palm Springs. His etheric spirits were working very hard for him and saved him because he was a good person.

———

Some stories are very sad because, as vulnerable humans, we are all flawed. A management client's retail firm had undergone a downturn with the falling economy. Jack arrived for our annual interview, but he didn't have taxes on his mind.

"Instead of me visiting my stores with promotions or sales announcements, I am now given the task of shedding employees all the time. I'm the bearer of bad news." Jack told me. He was a serious, likable person, but the Regional Manager's work had changed from success to survival mode.

Later that year, there were newspaper headlines about a murder-suicide. I was appalled to find out that it had been my client and I heard no more about it until the following year.

His son came to me for his father's joint tax returns from the last year. "He was intoxicated and had a fight with my mother. Then, he shot her and himself. I was completely surprised, and it was completely unexpected." He paused, and his voice became dark and unfriendly. "But the damn lawyers got involved when her family filed a wrongful death suit and they got all of the estate. They even came after me for some money I got from the household for the funeral. They said that I stole part of the estate and that there was no inheritance." He bitterly left with the parting statement, "Oh, charge whatever you want. It comes out of their money now!"

This is an example of how far-reaching personal problems can become when people succumb to alcohol and violence. There were no guardians or good spirits around to stop this violent end-of-life. Nothing but bitterness left behind for the heirs of a fine man who turned to murder.

It is worth mentioning the old statement that, "what comes around goes around". What this means is that a bad deed will be repaid in full. I have seen this many times, and it is worth keeping in mind that to be straight and honest with yourself and other people is the only course to peace and happiness. It is also worth mentioning that good deeds last forever, either in your memory or because people respect a good person, and nobody respects a thief or crook.

⌒

A very kind retired medical doctor named Samuel had been a hero in the Second World War. He was a corpsman with the Army Air Corps in Africa. They were bombing the Romanian oil fields held by the Germans. He observed that many of the neck wounds inflicted on the airmen in the bombers were from shrapnel coming from exploding anti-aircraft shells which penetrated the fuselage and Plexiglas. Sam took a helmet and designed a simple curtain of steel chainmail which hung from the edges. This was tested and found to be very efficient in stopping the shrapnel in the exposed neck area between the field jacket and helmet. One day, the doctor brought his military notebook with the pictures of him and the famous Army Air Generals and another amazing picture, which was taken through the open Bombay of the B- 17, which was flying at treetop level after dropping their bombs.

The good doctor went to medical school on the GI Bill after the war and, now, had retired to work part-time in a nursing home. He told me that he spent more time caring for the poor employees than the patients. When he was in his mid-90s, he found that he had used his life up. His hearing and sight were gone and unrepairable, his body was tired and not functioning well. He felt guilty as a burden to his daughter and husband who he lived with, now also senior citizens, for their support. He decided it was time to die and leave the world to make room for another person to take his place on the earth. He simply quit eating.

For five days, he didn't eat anything. Then, he peacefully passed away while still at home. He now rests in the care of Abraham and his God.

Recently, an elderly client named Lorraine spoke of her deceased husband. While he was ill in the later stages of his life, he would tell her that he had no belief in the afterlife, religious or not. He would pass simply away and that would be the end of his existence— no spirits or places in the hereafter. He had lived a simple life and retired from the Navy after 30 years to enjoy a peaceful period during retirement. His life would be fulfilled. Several years after he passed away, Lorraine fell asleep on the family room sofa after watching evening television. She startled and woke suddenly, sensing someone else was in the room. By the light of the television, she saw a familiar figure at the end of the sofa. It was her husband. He sat there looking at her, without expression or statement. He was a simply a ghost, appearing to give her a wordless greeting. Then, he vanished. Lorraine is convinced that he visited to show her that there is a hereafter and he wanted to let her know that he had been wrong.

When I came home from the Army, my parents, bride, and collie dog were waiting. Life was poor but happy with my mother's living room converted to our bedroom. My parents had a large house, but the top floor was rented out. Betty found a job with a department store nearby. She worked on the second floor and, sometimes, the dog would escape and visit. He would walk along the downtown sidewalk until he got to a crosswalk at the busy Main Street. There, a traffic policeman would halt the traffic and invite the dog to cross. The dog would bound across the street and visit his master who then would need to use her break to take the happy dog home again.

My brother finished his enlistment and visited the family before he moved out of state with his wife to a trucking job. My father would leave for work every day while my mother would be busy with housekeeping. She always kept the dog outside because she was a clean freak and dogs have lots of fur—collies especially.

One day, I was walking down the main street and saw Scottie on the other side. His head was down, and he was walking the same way as me. He didn't look up or acknowledge that he was following me. Finally, I stopped walking and yelled to him. He looked up and bounded across the street, looking innocently surprised. Time moved on and, after my son was born, we moved to a small apartment on the edge of town. The dog would get loose and visit us there. There are still scratches on the front door from his visits. I used to park my car behind the apartment, next to a fence near the main street. One day, my car was away for repairs and I was standing near the yard when I saw the collie coming down the street. He looked into the yard without seeing me or the car and turned around. It was then that I realized that he always looked for my car before he came to the door. I yelled to him and he ran joyfully to me.

We moved further away and didn't see the dog except when we visited my family. He was very lonely and chained to a post in the yard all the time. One day, my mother called and said Scottie was dead. He had been run over by a train. It was terrible news and I found it hard to believe because trains were nowhere near the house. The truth came out from my sister and the local newspaper. They reported that the collie had come onto the tracks as the train was approaching. He had looked at the train but did not move out of the way. The engineer hit the brakes but couldn't stop in time to avoid killing the dog. When he reported the accident, he stated that he thought the dog had deliberately put himself in harm's way as if he wanted to die. The dog had committed suicide.

The dog had died from loneliness. Loneliness is as deadly as poison to both people and animals. We all need love and companionship. Love must be returned.

This book could only have been completed because I have lived a long dangerous life and faced many thousands of people who had stories to tell. They were stories about mysterious forces and spirits that live amongst us quietly until needed. They are part of our extended silver thread soul and belong in the universe as surely as the huge oak trees in the forest. Native Indians know that our spirits abound long after our physical being has passed. They also know, as we are now discovering, that the earth and people are one. Like the arrow, we are both dependent on it for life, but it also brings death. Be aware of these forces of nature and how they can influence you and the loved ones around you. Pay attention to those dreams and loosen up to let the spiritual world visit. Tame your animal spirits and you will be astounded!

God Bless You All.

ABOUT THE NAVAJO CEREMONIAL TREE OF LIFE

Described by Steve Holt, a Comanche (from top to bottom)

Bars (on top): I believe these are Sacred Talking Sticks which have been used for centuries by many Native American tribes as a means of an orderly, just, and impartial hearing. Talking Sticks were most commonly used at major events such as tribal council meetings, pow- wow gatherings, and other important ceremonies. Their use was also extended to storytelling circles and teaching children. They allow people to present and express their sacred point of view.

Snow-covered Mountains: The first Navajo tribe emerged about 3,000 years ago at a point now called La Platte Mountain in Colorado. The four mountains sacred to the Navajo tribe were La Platte, Taylor, Navajo, and San Francisco, which were visually identified by different colors. The eastern mountains were white, the southern mountains were blue, the western mountains were yellow, and the northern mountains were black. The rise and fall of these mountains caused the alternation of day and night. When the white mountains rose, it was day, when the yellow mountains rose it was twilight, the black mountains brought night, and the blue mountains brought dawn.

Broken Arrows: Weapons no longer usable may connote a peace or the power of worship. Arrows represented both life and death for the Native Americans.

Tree: The Cherokee call trees "the Standing People" and teach that they are the givers of the Earth providing for the needs of others. Each tree has its own properties and attributes with the ability to share these with people-tree symbols. Trees provide healing medicine, shelter from the branches, a place for small animal burrows and provide materials to build homes. A tree symbolizes permanence, longevity, and its firm base symbolizes the concept of 'roots' and an ongoing relationship with natural surroundings. Such positive characteristics and attributes of trees lend themselves to be revered.

Bird Symbols are very special to the Native Americans: Their ability to soar above the clouds, perhaps to the heavens, and their sense of freedom inspires many. The many birds of North America are often featured in Native American art symbols, with many having different meanings to different tribes. However, because of their amazing power of flight, birds are almost always revered as bringers of messages and symbols of change across tribal differences.

Two Crows are near the top of the spiritual tree: In Native American folklore, the crow symbolizes wisdom. Many tribes believed that crows had the ability to speak and, therefore, considered them the wisest of the birds.

Light Brown Bird: This is a sparrow. Now, let me tell you Phil, this is no lie. Yesterday, a sparrow flew into my office and I helped it find its way out. Now, here I am writing about sparrows. The sparrow symbolism reflects the self-worth that each of us feels for ourselves regardless of external factors. The energy and passion for ourselves is within each of our hearts somewhere, waiting to be awakened. These little songbirds want us to sing our soul's own song, just as they do. In addition to inspiring us to love ourselves, the sparrow spirit also symbolizes the other joyful and caring qualities such as creativity, community, friendliness, and importance of simplicity.

White, Pink, and Brown Birds on lower branches: These are eagles or hawks. They look like birds of prey. The Eagle symbol signifies courage, wisdom, and strength. Its purpose was as the messenger to the Creator and as such was revered amongst the Bird Symbols. The Hawks are believed to continuously fly fighting, protecting people from the evil spirits of the air.

Horses are very powerful spiritually. Although the horse is present in many different cultures, with the Native Americans, they represent the same concepts of freedom and power. The horse is a symbol of freedom without restraint because riding a horse makes people feel they could free themselves from their own bindings. Also linked with riding horses, they are symbols of travel, movement, and desire. An important thing to remember about horses is that they are representatives of the spirit, similar to freedom. The horse serves man but can never be fully tamed by him. The horse represents power in Native American tribes. In the past Native American tribes that possessed horses often won more battles and obtained more territory than those who did not. The number of horses a tribe possessed was telling of how wealthy they were. Within these cultures and others, the horse is often an emblem of war.

White Horse: In some cultures, white horses stand for the balance of wisdom and power. In others, the white horse is a symbol of death. The white horse is the teacher of spiritual progress. It represents an avatar or master of knowledge and faith. They are adept in the fields of intellectualism and reason. They have command of their emotions and manifest unblemished justness. They signify the coming of spiritual lessons or teachers.

Brown Horse: The bay horse is a symbol of steady progress toward your goals. Know that you are safely on your path and nurturing all the right elements for yourself to grow. It is telling you to keep up the good work.

Turkey: He is on top of two sticks floating in a pool of water. The Navajo tribe believes that when all living creatures climbed to the bamboo stalk to escape the Great Flood, the wild turkey was on the lowest branch and his tail feathers trailed in the water. This is why the feathers of the turkey have no color—it was all washed out.

Goat: Goat's medicine includes abundance, independence, surefootedness, eliminating guilty feelings, understanding nature's energies and beings, seeking new heights, and agility.

Sheep: Don't say "baa" when you hear that, for Navajos, *Dine bi iina* means sheep is life, and calls for a celebration of sheep, wool, and weaving—all of it honoring the central role of sheep in Navajo spirituality and daily life, especially the endangered breed of Navajo-Churro sheep.

Navajo dancer on bottom: Celebrating life!

About the Author

Phillip Bruce Chute, EA is a businessman-writer. He lives with Nenita Lariosa, a retired educator, and is currently a tax and financial advisor with a consulting practice in Temecula, California. He has been an Enrolled Agent of the U.S. Treasury since 1976. While a professional tax expert, he practiced financial planning, stockbroker investments, and financial management for the clientele of his large tax practice. For 20 years he was a NASD licensed Registered Series 7, Registered Principal OSJ Series 24, and Financial Advisor Series 63. He currently holds California insurance licenses Fire & Casualty, Life & Disability, and Investment Annuities.

Phillip served as a paratrooper in the 82nd Airborne Division in the States and Europe during the Cold War. His financial career began when the State of California awarded him Private Investigator license #5912 as a business credit reporter for Dun & Bradstreet. Afterwards he worked as an accountant in various businesses until buying several practices in Riverside, California. The business evolved into a financial practice with a securities branch in Orange County, California.

Phillip has several other published works, including: *Stocks, Bonds & Taxes, The Metric Clock, Rock and Roll Murders*, and *American Independent Business*. He has also published articles for the *Nova Scotia* periodical, *The Shore News*.

The Author's Other Works

American Independent Business: His first book sold 5,000 copies and was used as a college textbook and reference for business entrepreneurs and is still available at 66 libraries. He's hard at work on a second version.

Rock & Roll Murders: Fiction, based on a true story about the KOLA radio station-Fred Cote Murder-One trials and conviction in Riverside of 1990.

The Metric Clock: Coming of Age Older Teen Fiction set in the mid-1940s New England.

Stocks Bonds and Taxes: Based on the authors 20 years as Securities Representative, Registered Principal OSJ, and Registered Investment Advisor. The material is provided by the author's investment client experience and by thousands of his tax clients.

Stocks, Bonds & Taxes: Textbook Edition: This version includes 330 questions to be used in college instruction.